D1270157

THE HOME UNIVERSITY LIBRARY
OF MODERN KNOWLEDGE
185

THE POET CHAUCER

The
Poet Chaucer

NEVILL COGHILL

FELLOW OF EXETER COLLEGE, OXFORD

LONDON
OXFORD UNIVERSITY PRESS
NEW YORK TORONTO

Oxford University Press, Amen House, London E.C.4

GLASGOW   NEW YORK   TORONTO   MELBOURNE   WELLINGTON
BOMBAY   CALCUTTA   MADRAS   KARACHI   LAHORE   DACCA
CAPE TOWN   SALISBURY   NAIROBI   IBADAN   ACCRA
KUALA LUMPUR   HONG KONG

First edition 1949
Reprinted (with Selected Reading
List) in 1950, 1955, 1960 *(with corrections) and* 1961

Printed in Great Britain by Butler & Tanner Ltd.,
Frome and London

TO MY MOTHER AND DAUGHTER

CONTENTS

ACKNOWLEDGEMENTS

I AM much under obligation to many friends for their patient reading of this book before it was printed, and for many wise and learned suggestions they have made and I have adopted. I offer them my best thanks, especially to Dr. R. M. Dawkins, Father Gervase Mathew, Mr. H. B. Barwise, Mr. H. V. Dyson, Sir William Halliday, Mr. Kenneth Sisam, and Professor Norman Davis.

INTRODUCTION

GEOFFREY CHAUCER is our greatest comic poet, and this study is an effort to discern the special gifts and accidents that made him so, ripening in him a full comic vision, at once essentially English and yet rooted in the whole culture of fourteenth-century Christendom.

It might be said that of all his gifts except that of an original genius the greatest was luck. Born in an age when our language was in solution but at a temperature to crystallize, Fortune chose him as the nucleus. Fortune disposed his birth in the right kind of family in the right part of England. Fortune sent him at the right moments to France and Italy, having elevated him to Court circles. And when other than poetical talents in him combined with this to ensure his positions of royal trust, and might have threatened his poetry with affluence and business, Fortune cast him down from favour a step or two (but not too far or for too long), leaving him with nothing to do but write *The Canterbury Tales*.

It is right to think of these as his greatest work, even if they do not reach so deeply into the heart of love as *Troilus and Criseyde*. But it is mistaken to treat them as a sudden and wholly unpredictable explosion of poetical power in a man who but for *Troilus* had only written minor poetry of little affinity with the *Tales*. It *was* an explosion, and it came late in his life, but the elements had long been preparing; his growth as a poet was gradual but unfaltering. So far as the chronology of his writings can be known or reasonably guessed, each successive poem showed the addition of some new power or craft, and the sum of these always remained with him, until he gave up writing altogether in the last few years of his life. For as long as he wrote, he retained a facility for calling on what was best in his earlier poetry to fashion or colour his maturest writing. In this he may be thought like Shakespeare but unlike Milton.

His poetical life can be considered as a kind of absorbed, yet sauntering journey from the ivory towers and high-walled gardens of medieval French imagination into the sun and humanism of the early Italian renaissance, and so home to the Tabard Inn, comfortably commonplace, as near the heart of English domestic life as Canterbury Cathedral in those days.

> And specially, from every shires ende
> Of Engelond to Caunterbury they wende . . .¹

And wherever he went he was reading from some book, comparing what he read with what he saw, learning to trust his eyes and his intelligence, and looking particularly at men and women, but with a glance cocked at their Universe, as it was then conceived. It was a progress from fantasy to actuality without loss of fantasy.

At the centre of his faculties of observation and feeling there was a wide-eyed affirmative wit that delighted in things for being what they were, especially when a little preposterous. And of all such objects, he regarded (or pretended to regard) himself as the most laughable. This is what gives the peculiarly 'Chaucerian' perspec-

---

¹ All quotations from Chaucer are taken from F. N. Robinson's edition published by the Oxford University Press, 1933. I have here and there added dots over a vowel to make scansion easier.

tive to his warm world. When at last he saw wickedness overbalance folly among the rogues that fascinated him, he shaded humour through ridicule into irony.

With his laughter there went a sensibility that is best called a power of pity,

> For pitee renneth soone in gentil herte.
> (*The Knight's Tale* and elsewhere)

His sense of beauty or delicacy was trained by the lucky accidents that placed and kept him in the rich elegances of royal and aristocratic life in Court or garden. We may discern a kindred sense in the gorgeous and exact taste of medieval miniature-painting, as in *Les Très Riches Heures du Duc de Berry* or the Wilton Diptych, the full-scale portrait of Richard II in Westminster Abbey, or the tapestries of *La Dame à la Licorne*. Chaucer was himself a great painter in words, and sees as easily with the eye of an Uccello as of a Tintoretto. He came at the beginning of portraiture and in the heyday of heraldry.

This essay tries to find the forms and qualities in his work, poem by poem, and to show how they are subtended, so to speak, from one to another; how the old merges with but is never quite lost in the new, and how almost all are built into *The Canterbury Tales*.

I could wish myself able to have shown these things in greater detail than I have, but he wrote many poems and this is but a short book. If it helps to turn attention towards the engendering as well as the flower, it will have done its work.

As luck played so large a part in the preparation of our first great poet, and went step by step with his poetry, I have divided what is known of his life (in so far as it can be seen to influence his writings) into brief sections, each, as I think, initiating a major phase in his luck. More is actually known of his doings in the world of affairs than I have thought necessary to include. Indeed a tolerably complete short biography of a trusted servant of the Court could be made out of the official records that, item by item, have come down to us about him, yet never mention him as a poet. What incidents in the life of a man of genius excite him to poetry are not always easy to see or guess, and only those are here included that make a sufficient continuity to be called a life and that have, as I think, a manifest effect upon his achievements in poetry.

One of these, his liquid music of language, noticed by Matthew Arnold, I have perhaps too much neglected. I have in a sense taken it for granted, but the truth is that although it pervades all his work it is less easy to demonstrate than his other qualities. Demonstration would involve not only some account of the language as it sounded six hundred years ago, but also the highly deterrent hieroglyphs of phonetic spelling, to represent it. And if these were accepted, there would still be the danger of all those vagaries of subjective and very often muddled judgements that so readily emerge when the precise values of this or that verbal sound in a given line of poetry are critically declared. There are many short and reliable guides to Chaucerian pronunciation, and those who try to read his poetry without at least a taste of it will soon become aware of what pleasures in sound they are missing. But the remedy is at their hand. For those who like music to their meaning, few poets can offer more than Chaucer.

1949

BIOGRAPHICAL (I)
(1340–1370)

IN OCTOBER 1386 a dispute as to the right to bear arms was heard before Sir John de Derwentwater in the Refectory of Westminster Abbey. The contestants were Sir Richard le Scrope and Sir Robert Grosvenor. One of the witnesses was Geoffrey Chaucer. With an agreeable and perhaps self-flattering vagueness he deposed that he was then 'forty years old and more', the sort of answer his own Pandarus, whom he had just created, might have given if asked so personal a question.

It seems therefore fair to infer that the poet was born in the early 1340s, and some such date would fit with the fact that he was on active military service in France—'in chyvachie' like the Squire in *The Prologue* to *The Canterbury Tales*—in 1359–60. He could hardly then have been much less than sixteen or seventeen. Those who like round numbers in the absence of positive information may place the poet's birth in 1340.[1]

He was born of parents not so obscure as to have left no record of their existence, nor so well-descended as in those days to rank as gentry. The family name goes back to the early thirteenth century in London and the Eastern Counties, but the first Chaucer known to have been related to the poet was his grandfather, Robert Chaucer, a collector at the Port of London of customs on wines from Aquitaine, in 1310. In about that year Robert's wife, Mary Heyroun, to whom he had been three years married, gave birth to a son and christened him John. This was the poet's father.

Little is recorded of John Chaucer, but that little is colourful. At the age of fourteen an attempted 'rape', as it was then called (but we would say 'abduction'), was made upon him, to marry him by force to one Joan de Westhale. Such outrages were then a not unusual way of securing family property. The marriage, however, was forestalled, and John survived a bachelor for some years. Later, at some unrecorded date after 1328, he married at his own choice. His wife was Agnes, daughter of James de Copton and niece of an official at the Mint. And it is she who is presumed to have been the mother of Geoffrey Chaucer the poet.

This was her second marriage. Her first husband had been William de Northwell, Keeper of the King's Wardrobe; so that what with these faint Court connexions and the appointment in 1348 of John Chaucer to be Deputy to the King's Butler at Southampton, there was a flavour of royal patronage as well as of wine about the family. Agnes, reviewing the advantages of her position, may well have decided on a Court career for her Geoffrey, then, let us suppose, about eight. If the Deputy Butler's boy could find a permanent post in a great household, he might even rise to being a Butler himself, with Deputies of his own.

Agnes and John were as fortunate as they were wise in their efforts to place young Geoffrey. They obtained for him the position of page in a household of royal rank, that of Lionel, Earl of Ulster, later Duke of Clarence, one of the sons of King Edward III. They may not have foreseen that this would prove an environment peculiarly favourable to the child's hidden gifts and qualities of temperament. It crowned his schooling, which he probably had at St. Paul's Almonry, in the Vintry, near where his father lived. The date of Geoffrey's elevation to the rank of page is not known, but it may confidently be placed in the early or middle fifties of the century, for the first historical record that mentions him by name is an entry in the household accounts of the Countess, Elisabeth, in 1357, itemizing payments for a paltock (an attenuated cloak), a pair of parti-coloured red-and-black breeches and a pair of shoes for him, together with twenty shilling 'for necessaries at Christmas'.

Apart from paltocks and parti-coloured breeches, there were other and more important things, not specified in the accounts, which the boy would have acquired in such a household: a code of Christian manners, elegant, affable and aristocratic (such as the Prioress took pains to counterfeit), and an appreciation of them in others; further study, indispensable to future advancement, of French and Latin, the tongues of Court and Church and culture; and an acquaintance, however distantly respectful with those Great Ones, the relatives and guests of the Countess. John of Gaunt, her brother-in-law, later to be the poet's most faithful patron, stayed at her Yorkshire seat at Hatfield when those red-and-black breeches were in their newest gloss. And in the following year (1358) the Countess graced a feast given on St. George's day by Edward III. There were present the Kings of France and Cyprus and the Queen of Scotland. Perhaps Geoffrey Chaucer was also in humble attendance.

While learning what was what in courtiership and running errands, one among a pack of pages better born in all probability than himself, Chaucer evaded the snares of snobbery though it was a quality he learnt to value in others for comic purposes. It is not unreasonable to believe he attracted favourable attention for his intelligence. To have passed, as he did in course of time from patron to patron and to be entrusted with increasing responsibilities in these high circles, proves that he knew his place and gave promise of willing aptitude. His poetry shows him the most intelligent and the most sensitive to courtliness of all our poets except perhaps Shakespeare, and indeed he may be thought to have had a hand in teaching the later poet, who loved his work, something of the romantic magnanimity of the noble folk we see in his earlier plays. The god-like manner and authority of Duke Theseus, patron of Bottom the Weaver, has much in common with Duke Theseus, arbiter of the fates of Palamon and Arcite.

The power of detailed observation seems to have been awake in Chaucer, even at this early age, in an ear for the niceties of North Country dialect. Years later he was to remember and place this kind of speech in the mouths of Aleyn and of John, the heroes of *The Reve's Tale.* The use of local dialect is now an accepted device in fiction. It was Chaucer who invented it. The London page, learning the language of gentlefolk, picked up that of the local peasantry simultaneously, and put it to comic use in the fullness of time with an originality as striking as his observation was precocious.

If his first adventure was to be raised from the wine-tubs of John and Agnes to the disciplines and excitements of a prince's household, his next adventure was in keeping with it and was another necessary step in the careers of page and poet. It was to go on service in the French wars.

Nothing is known of this service except that he was taken prisoner in 1359 or 1360, at 'Retters', so he deposed twenty-seven years later at the trial already referred to. Names change and memories are inaccurate. 'Retters' will be found on no map of France. It is thought to stand for Rhetel, near Rheims.

He has not told us who his captors were or how they treated him. He was a valuable prize, the servant of an earl at least, perhaps of the King. He was worth money; no doubt they treated him well. The ransom was paid on 1 March 1360. The King contributed £16.

The relative values of money from one age to another are subject to such fluctuations and calculated from scraps of evidence so variable and difficult to interpret that no accurate translation of what this would be worth in modern money is possible. As many of the items out of which Chaucer's biography has been reconstructed are concerned with payments, grants, and other financial transactions, it is useful to have some rule of thumb to compute such amounts in modern terms. To multiply by thirty or forty is the rule suggested by scholars in the subject. Edward III disbursed, therefore, something in the region of what would now count as £500 for his captive page.

Ransom and loot were two of the main emoluments of warfare at the time, and as a trapper avoids injury to the silver fox whose pelt he hopes to sell, so prisoners who were still the private property of their captors were treated with consideration, even with affection, if we may judge by the case of the young Count de Denia, who, captured by two Englishmen in service on one of the crazy wars of John of Gaunt, concealed himself, out of loyalty to them, as one of their servants when John of

B

Gaunt tried to claim the hostage as a Goverment prize. There is, then, no need to imagine chains and dungeons in Chaucer's case. It may even be reasonably conjectured that his captors were cultivated and friendly men, who, finding a lively and inquiring spirit in him, took pleasure in fascinating him with nice and romantic speculations on courtly love and by the loan of poems, such as the *Roman de la Rose*, in which that elegant and chastening system of erotics was delicately presented.

Geoffrey Chaucer had reached the right age for such things, ripe for poetical and amorous revelation. Whether it was then or later (and I cannot think it was much later) that he came upon the *Roman*, it was a major event in his life. We have his own word (in *The Legend of Good Women*) that he had at some time translated it, and part at least of his translation survives, though it cannot be dated with certainty. However, his first datable poem, *The Book of the Duchess* (1369–70), is so full of loving allusions and imitations from the *Roman* and other French poems in the same manner, that it seems certain he had been already long possessed by them. The ten years between his capture and *The Book of the Duchess* may well have been the years during which his translation of the *Roman* was in progress. He was at work on other translations too and on imitative poems of his own.

Meanwhile he was growing into a courtier, in attendance on King Edward III or on his son the Duke of Clarence.[1] The Duke was in Ireland between 1361 and 1366, and it may be that Chaucer was with him, for there is no record of his being employed elsewhere during those years. If so, it was the only foreign country he ever visited that left no mark upon his poetry.

[1] Created Duke of Clarence, 1362.

In 1366 his father died and his mother married for the third time, on this occasion to one Bartholomew atte Chapel, and with that she disappears from the story. Neither of his parents figures in his poetry. It is probable that in this year he, too, married. His bride was Philippa, daughter of Sir Payne Roet and sister of Katharine Swynford, sometime mistress and later third wife to John of Gaunt. Philippa was a lady in attendance on the Queen, from whom she had an income of ten marks a year. Nothing is known of their courtship, and almost nothing of their life together. Such allusions to it as Chaucer chose to make in his poetry are tinged with irony, and this has often been interpreted as evidence of unhappiness between them. I think it possible that they rubbed along together well enough for him to permit himself occasional jokes of a conventional kind at her expense and at the expense of the married state.

It is unwise to say more of their marriage than that it must have commended itself to them in frequent meetings about the Court and that it was an excellent match for both of them from the worldly point of view. If one considers the humbleness of the Chaucer family, on the fringe of Court but well below the salt, to marry a Roet, so well placed herself and the sister of greatness, was a step up for Geoffrey; one might almost call it an alliance. Philippa on the other hand had gained a young and promising husband apparently in the way of steady promotion. In the following year (1367) the King granted him an annuity of twenty marks and described him as 'dilectus valettus noster'. He was now a full valet, carrying candles before the King, making his bed and attending to a variety of duties, some of which were beginning to look like affairs of State. In 1368 and 1370 he was sent abroad on diplomatic or commercial business for the Crown. He was a coming young man. His income, combined with Philippa's, though small was not inconsiderable, amounting to something in the region of £350 of our money; and there were presents and perquisites. It was a competence.

Chaucer was now established in the world, married, and on the road to an indefinite advancement in public affairs, intelligent, educated, and giving evidence of aptitude in negotiation. It may be thought he was unusually likeable, especially to men, because of his wide conversational interests and lively fund of unexpected knowledge. As to women, it is less safe to conjecture. He has the whim in his poetry to represent himself as most unlikely to attract them. This may well be true. He knew too much about them.

Meanwhile he was growing as a poet no less certainly than as a courtier. If in the latter capacity his *primum mobile* was Edward III and his sons, in his capacity as a poet it was the *Roman de la Rose* and a gardenful of other French poetry in the same vein.

Postscript on the date of Chaucer's birth

Quoting from the opening paragraphs of this chapter, Mr. D. S. Bland in the *Times Literary Supplement* of 26 April, 1957, sought to argue that the phrase I have translated as 'forty years old and more' (*del age de xl ans & plus*) had the stricter, legal meaning of 'over forty but not yet forty-one'. A correspondence followed, concluded by a letter from Mr. G. D. G. Hall (28 June), who showed that the phrase was not necessarily open to so precise an interpretation in a legal document of this character and that to accept it would involve us in the belief that Chaucer was sent to France on active service at the age of thirteen, which, as Mr Hall remarks, 'is possible, though unlikely'.

2

GRADUS AD PARNASSUM

FROM THE beginning Chaucer knew how to yield himself to a book. He can be studied as a great reader no less than as a great writer. He seems to have read with an excited veneration, on the brink of wonder, and yet with a tempering of common sense, so that the wonder would often edge towards a veiled incredulity, if that is not too strong an expression for his delicate doubts.

Books to him were generally 'olde bokes'; that is, a reverence was due to them for their antiquity. They were the gathered wisdom and memory of the world:

> And yf that olde bokes were aweye,
> Yloren [1] were of remembraunce the keye.
>   (BF. [2] Prol. *The Legend of Good Women*)

For this reason they constituted what he called '*Auctoritee*', and this he found liable to be in conflict with '*Experience*'. It is one of the major antitheses in all Chaucer's thought and a recurring ingredient in his finest touches of wit and can openly be seen in *The Wife of Bath's Prologue*:

> Experience, though noon auctoritee
> Were in this world, is right ynogh for me
> To speke of wo that is in mariage . . .

or in a shadowier more ironical way in the opening lines of *The Legend of Good Women*. Indeed he has many passages contrasting or at least comparing what can be learnt from books and from the naked eye.

[1] Lost.   [2] See page 94.

Nothing except a May morning, he tells us, gave him greater pleasure than a book. What he read seemed effortlessly to store itself in an almost faultless verbal memory. Throughout his works phrase upon phrase, passage upon passage, have been found which, taken by him from their old context in some forgotten poem or philosophical work, he turned into Chaucerian poetry. He had assimilated them and they lived in a prompt memory, ready to emerge at the right moment in their Chaucerized form. What we memorize we love, for memory makes it a part of ourselves and therefore, to us, an object of love.

No book except the Bible was more continually present to his imagination than the *Roman de la Rose*.

This book, a manuscript of which must often in these years (1360–70) have lain before him, was the work of two very different men and it would be hard to say which of them had the more profound effect upon him, the one immediately, the other by delayed action. For the rest of his life they were to hover like angels, romantic and satiric, at either side of his imagination. The first was Guillaume de Lorris and the second Jean Clopinel ('club-foot') de Meun.

Guillaume was the original author who began, but never completed, his poem, towards the year 1237. He was then in or about his twentieth year, full of grace, amorousness, and the flourish of youth. After composing some four and a half thousand lines he broke off, leaving his story half told. Forty years later the limping cynic Jean de Meun added a coda, a devil's tail of eighteen thousand lines, to the simple, sensuous, and passionate body of Guillaume's work.

Where love and girlhood were concerned, no Pre-

Raphaelite, not even Tennyson himself, was more rosily
moved than Guillaume. To Jean de Meun, however,
women were what fools were to Croker. They were
'meat and drink to him'. All that Chaucer has to say
of girls and gardens, and he has much that is lovely to
say of both, is a fresh evocation of the Garden of the
Rose imagined by Guillaume:

> So fair a gardyn woot I nowher noon.
> For, out of doute, I verraily suppose
> That he that wroot the Romance of the Rose
> Ne koude of it the beautee well devyse. . . . .
>   (*The Merchant's Tale*)

And whatever Chaucer ventures in humorous denigra-
tion of women, their subtle shifts, their manners drunk or
sober, their innocence real or pretended, their costliness
and general suitability as objects of love, is grounded in
the cynicism of Jean de Meun. Guillaume and Jean
were complementary; their collaboration, if such it can
be called, was a union of opposites. The balance of their
day and night is ever present in Chaucer's work, his
earlier is drenched in sunlight, his maturest is after night-
fall with a twinkle of frost.

There are three fragments, comprising nearly 7,700
lines, translated from the *Roman* and generally printed
(ever since the first collected edition of William Thynne
in 1532) among Chaucer's writings. Whether all or any
of these fragments is his authentic work is still a matter
of dispute. The arguments advanced are philological
rather than literary and the balance of scholarly opinion
inclines to the view that the first of them at least is
Chaucer's own. If the remaining fragments were by
another hand, it was a hand hardly less skilful than his.

There are few translations in English that are so fresh, so easy, and so accurate.

The *Roman de la Rose* begins as an allegory, entered by way of a dream, and expands into an encyclopedia of medieval learning, during the exhibition of which the main story, of the Lover striving to reach and pluck the rose of Love, is lost sight of for hundreds of lines at a time. At the very end, however, Jean de Meun remembered the young hero and allowed him the happy ending no doubt designed by Guillaume de Lorris, an ending which, if Jean de Meun's attitude to the female sex is to be trusted, may not have been so happy after all. Anyhow he plucks his rose.

Allegory was a normal and indeed dominant habit of thought, and especially of poetic thought, in the middle ages. It had an elaborate technique of interpretation, and, like a fugue in music, is based on a theme pursued harmoniously on several planes, each with a 'meaning' of its own. There is the literal sense of the story as such, in which the theme is seen as narrative, the allegorical sense in which it appears as a transference of our own nature or situation into typical or personified terms, and the moral sense expressed in maxims of conduct, illustrable no less from the narrative than from our own lives.

Thus in the *Roman*, the theme is love-longing seen in the lingering narrative of a young man seeking to pluck a rose in a dreamy garden. The garden is peopled with abstract personifications who help or hinder his desire, and these are embodiments of our own spiritual or psychological impulses and create the typical situations of the course of true love. Positive injunctions and prohibitions are added as maxims for the behaviour of lovers, and the whole is so blended and embellished as to create a unified imaginative experience.

This rich way of multiple but simultaneous thought was by no means confined to poetry. It was a normal way of comment on biblical texts in popular sermons, capable of such refinements of suggestion as to produce what seem to us the very acrobatics of interpretation. In philosophic and scientific inquiry the method was in harmony with the doctrine of the macrocosm and the microcosm which held that the Universe was reflected or echoed in the particulars of creation, and that valid arguments and interconnexions could be discovered to explain one in terms of the other.

Thus allegory was not, as some have thought, a tiresome literary trick, but an oblique way of conveying important mysteries, intuitions, passions, qualities, and feelings, the very business of poetry itself; not only of poetry but of all fine art, as we can see from tapestries, carvings, and manuscript illuminations of those ages.

The accepted approach of poetry to this figurative instruction was through a dream and this was very natural, for they also believed, as we do, that actual dreams could be mirrors in which the dreamer's spiritual condition was to be discerned. Four of Chaucer's poems took this road into the imaginative world.

What is it like to be in love? What does the experience mean? What does it do to us? What ought we to do about it? It may be that there are direct answers to such questions. Guillaume de Lorris preferred the slanted approach of dream-allegory. To him it was like being in a garden on a May morning. The garden was safely enclosed by an embattled wall, hung, on the outer side, with effigies of all those things that were never to be permitted to enter it, scarecrows hung up to frighten off their own kind . . . hatred, ill-breeding, meanness, hypocrisy, envy, old age, sorrow, and poverty. These had no part in love.

Love was for the young, the generous, for those of courtesy and 'sweet-looking'; above all, for the beautiful. *Mirth* was the maker and Lord of this garden, and *Idleness* she who was appointed to open the wicket in the wall by which the dreamer entered it. There he was to find the timeless and leisurely children of honour who, in their fresh beauty and gladness, dance their formal dances in the sun, or play in pairs on the soft grass under shady trees, laden with spices. To be in love confers a kind of aristocracy upon the lover; a nature capable of the one is capable of the other.

There are few surprises in what Guillaume thought to be the constituents of human beauty. The girls are golden-haired like *Idleness*, bright as a basin newly scoured; their flesh is soft and smooth and flower-like; their eyes grey, and widely set under slender arching brows; their features are small and neat, the mouth small, soft and sweet of breath, set above a cloven chin, the nose 'tretys', shapely. All this delicate fashion of beauty, after so many years, so often repeated, may now seem insipid and banal; but in Guillaume and his translator there is a profound enjoyment of these simplicities. The young men do not seem to fascinate him so much; he spends less time on their description. *Mirth* is one; he also has grey eyes and a 'metely mouth', is broad of shoulder and slender of waist. He has no beard but his hair is crisp and shining. His samite garment, above and below, is slashed for wantonness,

> Al toslytered for queyntise.[1]

---

[1] Slashed for fantasy.

Youth has a friend who kisses her without concealment upon impulse; she is

> With herte wylde, and thought volage,[1]

and he is of the same disposition. It is something of a shock to learn that they are both twelve years of age; but then Shakespeare's Juliet was thirteen, and Guillaume was a Latin.

Music and dance, the song of many birds, the long sunlight, the grass, 'as soft as any velvet', the peaches, the cinnamon, the maples, the waterways, the wells that have no frogs in them, the periwinkles and the violets are in the long catalogue of love-pleasures in this protected garden where the squirrels, the roes, and the conies play among enamoured abstractions from the game of love, such as those I have named, *Idleness, Mirth, Youth,* and the rest. It is a setting that we have learnt to associate with the French genius, the music of Couperin, the tapestries of Boucher; it is the cult not so much of women as of femininity itself. Like Dresden china, it may seem preposterous, but it is very pretty; it is as natural as it is artificial, a dream that is a picture of the longings of love. Chaucer loved the preposterous before he laughed about it.

In every game all possible situations within it are foreseen and controlled by rules and conventions. So with the game of Love; having mustered his court cards on his velvety table, Guillaume next indicated how the game was to be played, codifying it into something like a philosophy. As this code is so often to be pre-supposed in Chaucer, some of the simpler rules may here be taken, partly from the *Roman* and partly from other sources for the cult of courtly love.

[1] Volatile.

First as to the experience of love itself. It is the sudden
wound of joy and torment that sexual beauty makes on
refined male sensibility, a great anguish, an ecstasy, a
kind of death in love at first sight, an arrow to the heart.

> Your yën two wol slee me sodenly;
> I may the beautee of hem not sustene,
> So woundeth hit thourghout my herte kene.
> *(Merciless Beauty)*

This causes the lamentation invariable in a young
Chaucerian lover, for such an experience is an irretriev-
able and exquisite disaster, for which there is no cure
but the unlikely perhaps impossible compliance of the
lady. Why indeed should she comply with the desires of
a wretch, prostrate at her shrine, to which he dare not
so much as lift his hand, a creature in whom a conviction
of his utter unworthiness was born in the same moment
as his sense of her unapproachable perfections?

Love of this kind constrains him to her service, but
unconditionally. He is not forbidden to hope for his
reward but he cannot expect it. Nor can he make a
demand by right upon her; even after long service of
which she may be quite unconscious, mercy is as much
as he can ask, and to say that one word '*Mercy!*' is in
Chaucer the characteristic form of a lover's declaration
of his passion. It is the word used by the Man in Black
in *The Book of the Duchess*, it is the last word of Arcite
in *The Knight's Tale*, the first word of Damian to May in
The Merchant's Tale, the word of Aurelius to Dorigen in
The Franklin's Tale, the word round which the love of
Troilus is built.

As these last three examples show, the essential nature
of this love is that it is illicit and even adulterous.
Marriage is not its object. It is the heart's entreaty for a

mistress, not for a wife. This fact is not to be explained on the basis of libertinism but on a piece of strict logical casuistry. Christian marriage, a sacrament undertaken with a view to the propagation of children, is also a contract in which the wife promises obedience to her husband; she cannot refuse him without breaking her vow. He is one

> That hath hir body whan so that hym liketh.
> *(The Franklin's Tale)*

Marriage would destroy love, not by slackening mutual desire, but by reversing the order of things. The suppliant and servant would become the lord and master; consequently the lady could bestow no favour that was not his by right already. She would not be free. Personal freedom in Chaucer means open-handedness, generosity, one of the highest qualities of a noble nature. It is listed with truth, honour, and courtesy as the first attributes of the Knight in *The Prologue* to *The Canterbury Tales*, and is a perfection that a lady worthy of love should have. Matrimony, where there is no sexual 'freedom', would deprive her of it by taking away the divine power of bestowing 'grace'.

There was no time-limit set to the service of the lover. Little wonder that one caught in the delicate mesh of so fantastic a system should bewail his lot, refuse his food, and lie awake weeping at night, inditing 'complaints'.

Servant to the whim of his mistress, the lover has also the commands of Cupid to obey. He must be faithful and secret, her honour and the honour of all women must be his first consideration. He must bear his pain with a smile in public, lest his love should be suspected and thus open his mistress to the 'wicked tongues' of scandal. One sworn friend he may have, and no more, to whom he may disclose his passion. This is the only solace he has by right, and this friend must do what he can to advance his cause with his lady. The lover must by all means shun 'villainy', that is, low-born behaviour, cruelty, violence, ribald speech, and churlishness. He must keep himself from pride and yet have great care of his appearance, in the cut of his clothes, the whiteness of his teeth, the cleanness of his fingernails. He must flee avarice and niggardliness, tell no lies, keep chaste, and extort nothing from an unwilling love. Nor may he subvert the love of any pair already happy in each other. Noble birth is not necessary to him, for love is not a matter of lineage (as marriage for the most part was) but of fine behaviour. Love confers nobility and those capable of experiencing it are nature's noblemen. They are generous, brave, compassionate, humble, capable of friendship, dependable. Such were the chief virtues conferred by courtly love, taming and civilizing the healthy male, and for these virtues it was esteemed even though it was recognized at the same time to be sinful when they thought as Christians.

The conventional lady, for her part, was a complex of yielding and withdrawal. She must above all be beautiful and chaste in heart, that is, not given to other men, nor indeed too easily to her chosen lover.[1] The qualities of pity, welcomingness, and bounty of soul (what is called 'Franchise') will move her towards the lover. But she must also be shamefast and guarded by a sense of *Danger* (Disdain), and fear the loss of her

[1] But the authorities are not unanimous on this point. Andreas Capellanus esteems willingness to grant the thing desired as one of the qualities in a lady that make her desirable.

reputation by the discovery of her love. These will give her pause in yielding; but once yielded, constancy and faith is as much demanded of her as of her lover.

Opposed as it was to accepted Christian morality, courtly love had evolved a system and terminology derived from Christian ideas, and its exaltation of women may not be unconnected with the growing reverence paid to the person of the Blessed Virgin. The parallelism between the religion of Christ and the religion of Cupid is seen in expressions common to both, such as conversion, penance, service, prayer, fasting, martyrdom, sanctity, faith, works, and hope in the lover; in the lady, grace, pity, mercy, stableness, and so forth. The experience of love can only have one language, whether it be a human love or a divine,[1] and just as the theorists of courtly love borrowed the terms of catholic thought for their system, so the writers of many a lovely hymn to the Virgin and to Christ in this age borrowed the language of erotic poetry with no sense of incongruity, as can be seen from such a poem as that addressed to the Blessed Virgin, which has the refrain *Quia amore langueo*.

Nevertheless, lovers and poets, and theoreticians like Andreas Capellanus, who wrote about the nature of courtly love and from whose work much of the foregoing account of its nature is taken, were acutely conscious that earthly love as they had formulated it was held damnable as sin, *sub specie aeternitatis*, that is, in the heavenly world. Here was a dilemma upon which the middle ages found itself impaled. How could such a love be good if it were forbidden by God? How could it be evil if it were the nurse to so many virtues?

[1] So in Titian's painting *Sacred and Profane Love*, it is a question to some which is which.

The middle ages were exceedingly logical; debate, to the point of hair-splitting, was one of their special pleasures. We are accustomed to thinking of French civilization as pre-eminent for a conception of reason, and civilization as Chaucer knew it was largely French. But although logic had spun these refinements of theory round the newly discovered passion of romantic love, distinguishing it so sharply from anything that could or ought to be in marriage, yet even so an intuition how these irreconcilables—love and marriage—could be combined in common sense was to shape itself in Chaucer's mind. Popular romance and fairy tale tended to lead their heroes and heroines after all adventures to a sanctified and bridal bed, but in such tales the emphasis was on epic or magic rather than on romantic love and its special problems. Chaucer with his clear-thinking mind came to turn Boccaccio's epic of Theseus into the Loves of Palamon and Arcite in *The Knight's Tale*, and saw at the end that Emily's power to bestow love upon her servant Palamon must somehow be squared with the fact that he became her lord in marriage, and thus he attempts it: I have italicized the happy solution.

> For now is Palamon in alle wele . . .[1]
> And Emelye hym loveth so tendrely,
> *And he hire serveth al so gentilly,*
> That nevere was ther no word hem bitwene
> Of jalousie or any oother teene.[2]

This was the germ of the final arrangement he found for Dorigen and Arveragus in *The Franklin's Tale*. Dorigen

> Hath swich a pitee caught of his penaunce

---

[1] In all happiness.   [2] Any other trouble.

that she consented to take him for her husband and her lord

> Of swich lordshipe as men han over hir wyves,

while her husband, Arveragus, on his part, swore her as a knight that he

> Ne sholde upon hym take no maistrie
> Agayn hir wyl, ne kithe [1] hire jalousie,
> But hire obeye, and folwe hir wyl in al,
> As any lovere to his lady shal,
> Save that the name of soveraynetee,
> That wolde he have for shame of his degree. . . .
> Thus been they bothe in quiete and in reste.

This humane solution he was to reach in his later life. For the moment, however, he was young and captivated by the principles of Guillaume de Lorris who had no thought of marriage in his *Roman de la Rose*. Chaucer was still a beginner in love as in poetry and before he came to declare himself as a modest expert in both he set himself to learn and abide by the traditional rules. It was enough for the moment that he had Guillaume's gospel and decalogue of love before him, a musical chime of syllables and a poetic form of dream and allegory to teach him an art for the service of lovers and for all who 'die like a rose in aromatic pain'. The young courtier's first military expedition to France was a step forward in his career as a servant of royalty; it was an even longer step forward into the civilization that Europe was creating. If the Hundred Years War did nothing else for us it sent Chaucer to France, and brought him back again with the first of the keys of European poetry in his pocket.

[1] Show.

C

3

POEM FOR A PATRON

IN THE ten years between his ransoming and his first poem of known date, *The Book of the Duchess*, Chaucer was slowly reaching saturation-point in French poetry; at any moment the liquor must re-distil itself into his own tongue. Apart from the *Roman*, he had many other models out of France, especially in the poems of Guillaume de Machault and Guillaume de Deguilleville, and Jean Froissart. At some time during these years he wrote at least one notable poem that we still have, an alphabet of prayer to Our Lady, taken from Deguilleville and made more beautiful by freedoms of his own. Chaucer had special feeling for the Blessed Virgin, seen at its sweetest in the Tales of the Prioress and the Man of Law; here in early years, the same feeling, expressed a little more stumblingly, is in his lines:

> Moises, that saugh the bush with flawmes rede
> Brenninge, of which ther never a stikke brende,
> Was signe of thin unwemmed [1] maidenhede.
> Thou art the bush on which ther gan descende
> The Holi Gost, the which that Moyses wende [2]
> Had ben a-fyr; and this was in figure. [3]
> Now, ladi, from the fyr thou us defende
> Which that in helle eternalli shal dure.

The exquisite turning of the conceit (from one kind of fire to another) in the last two lines was an adornment of Chaucer's own, not in the original, and shows the

[1] Unspotted.   [2] Supposed.
[3] This was an allegory.

true nature of a pun; namely, that it is, like allegory itself, a way of thinking two thoughts at once, whose double action opens the mind with surprise to something almost more than it can so quickly hold, as do the best of Shakespeare's puns.

To say that *The Book of the Duchess* has a primrose freshness is only half its praise. It also has the formal beauty of demeanour that springs from a loving obedience to exact conventions. It is almost as strict poetically as a fine shield is strict heraldically; the colours and shapes are determined in advance and meticulously placed, and just as a herald can precisely blazon an achievement, so a critic could blazon this poem,

'On a field of dream, melancholy, a May morning, azure, between trees and flowers, proper, a lover, sable, and a poet, passant, regardant; a canton of Ovid with bird-song in chief.'

All the conventions are there. And just as an escutcheon, painted by a master-herald, is bright and proportionable so that the arms, however familiar, seem freshly new, so this poem compounded of so many conventions has an untarnished novelty and living grace.

A convention becomes natural by second nature. Its ingredients may be learnt and assembled laboriously, as a beginner may learn and assemble the words of a foreign language to compose a sentence; but until the grammar and vocabulary have become a part of him, his use of it will not seem natural, he will be translating his thoughts rather than thinking them spontaneously in the acquired tongue. There are some who never reach this spontaneity. Chaucer pre-eminently had the faculty of grafting to his own nature the conventions of foreign poetries, and the whole consequent harvest of his work retains the form and flavour of European culture, absolutely assimilated to his personal genius. Langland was an islander, but Chaucer was a European.

The Book of the Duchess is an occasional poem, an elegy on the bereavement of an English Duke. Yet it is so truly in the main stream of romance tradition that it not only embodies many of the earlier conventions of French poetry, but also in a sense prophesies the work of at least one great Italian painter, Uccello, not yet born when Chaucer was writing it, and who indeed can never have known the poem. Nevertheless one of his paintings might be taken as an illustration of it as will be seen presently.

An outline of the narrative is easily given: sleepless for love, which, he says, has held him eight years captive, the poet reaches for a book 'to drive the night away'; it is the *Metamorphoses* of Ovid. There he reads the tale of Ceix and Halcyon, and he then re-tells it in his own simple and touching manner; after which he successfully invokes the god of sleep and falls into a dream, 'inly sweet', that it was a May morning wakening him with the song of birds and the horns of hunters. In his dream, he rises, takes horse, and joins the hunt among the trees of a forest. There he comes upon a man in black, leaning sorrowfully against an oak tree, and speaking a sad poem about his lady. Chaucer falls into conversation with him and the Man in Black gradually discloses the cause of his grief, that it is for his lady whom he had faithfully served, wooed, and at last won. He describes her person and the beauty of her character, and finally reveals that the grief he suffers is for her death. Almost at once the castle bell tolls twelve through his dream and Chaucer, awakened by it, finds the book of Ceix and Halcyon still beside him;

This was my sweven; [1] now hit ys doon.

The Book of the Duchess is the first and best of his longer poems in the French kind (except, perhaps, the Prologues to *The Legend of Good Women*) and for all its conscious borrowings and echoes, it is digested in his own manner and points towards his own poetical future.

It has faults or at least falterings; though the sequence of lyrical and elegiac mood is never broken it is spun, here and there, a little thin. There are lines unskilful and naïve and the display of learning is a little mechanical; yet it is an evening's reading of a pure and steady pleasure, not in the verses alone or even in the ebb and flow of courtly feeling, but also in the shaping of the fable; the design is delicate and sufficient. The poem fulfills itself.

Dr. Johnson has said of *Lycidas* and of the pastoral form of poetry that 'where there is leisure for fiction there is little grief'; but this is not true. To evade or to decorate the sorrow of bereavement seems an almost universal instinct, not only among the poets, but in common life. Nodding plumes, solemn music, and even such phrases as 'he passed away' for 'he died', show our habitual impulses to escape out of the natural violence of grief into some formal beauty or euphemism, through which sorrow may be contemplated rather than experienced. And this is the nature of elegiac poetry.

Chaucer chose a dream to decorate this death, and his setting for the chief mourner, the Man in Black, is the freshness of a May morning and a woodland hunt. This

[1] Dream.

is the paradox of originality in the midst of conventions;
it is to place loss where it can best be seen, in a ring of
joy and daybreak, not in September when the Duchess
died. It is the time of sport and of lovers in the freshen-
ing year. Such was Chaucer's first fiction, much like one
of the earliest of Shakespeare's in *Love's Labour's Lost*,
where, at the height of a summer merriment, the black
figure of Mercadé enters to tell the Princess and her lover
of her father's death. Allegory can find no better setting
for death than in the midst of life.

But if *The Book of the Duchess* is a poem celebrating a
death it also celebrates a love; and in this it points
forward to much of Chaucer's future poetry and to
the man who was to describe himself as one

> That helpeth loveres, as I kan, to pleyne.
> *(Troilus and Criseyde, I)*

So the mood of this allegory is as much lyrical as elegiac
and it begins with the poet's own sleeplessness for a long
love, never requited.

> For there is phisicien but oon
> That may me hele; but that is don.
> Passe we over untill eft; [1]
> That wil not be mot nede [2] be left.

Love-sickness and 'default of sleep' led him naturally to
Ovid,

> To rede, and drive the night away,

and the spell of a mood of lovers' melancholy, of bereavement and of constancy in grief is fully cast by the end of
the tale of Ceix and Halcyon.

> With that hir eyen up she casteth
> And saw noght. 'Allas!' quod she for sorwe,
> And deyede within the thridde morwe.

---

[1] Afterwards.   [2] What will not be must needs.

In this tale, so well-matched to the theme of the death of Blanche, that art of story-telling in which we have come to think Chaucer supreme is first displayed. His classical narrative of Ceix and Halcyon has a naturalness preferred by Dryden to the artifice of Ovid, and yet another touch that we now call Chaucerian, the touch of humour. Juno sends a messenger to awake the god of sleep couched in a cave where water

> Came rennynge fro the clyves adoun,
> That made a dedly slepynge soun,

and the god of sleep lay snoring to admiration.

> This messager com fleynge faste
> And cried, 'O, ho! awake anoon!'
> Hit was for noght; there herde hym non.

When he has finished reading the tale of Ceix and Halcyon Chaucer thinks back to this god of sleep, and uses him to advance his own fable that he himself is sleepless for love, by promising the god

> Yif he wol make me slepe a lyte,
> Of down of pure dowves white
> I wil yive hym a fether-bed.

And in a trice upon this jest, the poet is asleep and entering upon that dream which is at once purely conventional and wholly personal. Dreams were to be perpetual matter for Chaucer's later poetry: dreams feigned, so as to start a poem; allegorical dreams, such as Criseyde had, to show the state of her feelings; dreams that come of indigestion, and prophetic dreams that seem to involve a theory of predestination: all were to return again and again in his writing. Poetry, psychology, medicine, and theology had so much to say of them, and these were sciences in which Chaucer was well versed.

˥ But perhaps the most striking feature in *The Book of the Duchess*, a trick (if trick it can be called) that he was to use in every major poem except *Troilus and Criseyde*, was the introduction of himself as a character in the poem.

This is the first of his many appearances as a simpleton, a man of unsuccess but of excellent good will, an asker of foolish questions and not a great giver of wise answers. Later in *The House of Fame* such a Chaucer was to appear and be lectured and patronized by a bird, in *The Canterbury Tales* by a publican. This great device of the laugh against oneself, seems to me one, if not a chief, source of all his humour. It combines a certain prominence of self with an endearing modesty. It can be used to give a flavour of *naïveté*, or, if need be, of subtle comment preposterous, ironical, serious, or sly. And in *The Book of the Duchess* it is combined with another of his best gifts as a writer, the gift of being able to write an easy naturalistic and broken conversation in rhymed verse. This gift is seen at its highest point in English in *Troilus and Criseyde* and *The Canterbury Tales*, but its first manifestation is in this early elegy for a patroness.

> 'By oure Lord,' quod I, 'y trowe yow wel!
> Hardely,[1] your love was wel beset;
> I not how ye myghte have do bet.'
> 'Bet? ne no wyght so wel,' quod he.
> 'Y trowe hyt,' quod I, 'parde!'
> 'Nay, leve hyt wel!' 'Sire, so do I . . . '.[2]

---

[1] Frankly.
[2] 'By our Lord,' said I, 'I can well believe you.
Certainly your love was well bestowed;
I don't know how you could have done better.'
'Better? No one could have done so well,' said he.
'By God I believe it, Sir,' said I.
'No, but trust it truly!' 'Sir, so I do.'

Conversation was an art much esteemed in the four-teenth century. Copiousness and fluency of conversation come third, after personal beauty and honesty of behaviour (*probitas morum*), among the five chief causes of love listed by Andreas Capellanus; and here, in *The Book of the Duchess*, the Man in Black singles out among the high qualities of his lady, 'her goodly, softe speche'.

> So frendly, and so well ygrounded,
> Up al resoun so wel yfounded,
> And so tretable to alle goode
> That I dar swere wel by the roode,
> Of eloquence was never founde
> So swete a sownynge facounde.[1] . . .

Chaucer was one of the first poets to put credible con-versation into poetry, and he did it in this his first poem. Love, humour, dream-lore, narrative power, the modest presence of the poet, and a natural way of talking are all intertwined here, and are some of the things that were to shape the future of his poetry and endow it with those qualities that we now recognize as distinctively 'Chaucerian'.

Chaucer's debt to his French models was not simply a matter of borrowing such large features as the dream, the May morning, the birdsong, the woodland flower-scapes, and the melancholy lover, which make the machinery of the poem. He foraged also for detail in Machault, Froissart, and the *Roman de la Rose* with the excitement of a plunderer in El Dorado. In *The Book of the Duchess* are embedded the lesser nuggets of verbal theft, taken and

---

[1] So friendly and so well grounded and founded upon reason, so inclinable to all good that I dare swear by the rood there was never found so sweet and fluent a sound of eloquence.

translated (naturally without acknowledgement) from poems whose names are 'five sweet symphonies' and more. The *Paradis d'Amour*, the *Remède de Fortune*, the *Jugement du Roi de Behaigne*, the *Lay de Confort*, the *Dit du Lion*, and the *Fontaine Amoureuse*, are some of them. Scholarship has found many parallels, some indeed are so truly parallel that they seem never to meet. A study of Chaucer's poem with so great an array of evidence that he was a thief in poetry invites two questions: what was his method of work? Had he no shame?

These French poems are all such as would be called 'long'. The *Roman de la Rose* would pass for 'long' in any age; nor was it neatly printed in a convenient book. It stretched through many a bulky page of parchment. What a pile of paper must have lain on Chaucer's desk if we imagine him surrounded (as the evidence of verbal thefts suggests) by so many tributary manuscripts! It may be that from time to time he refreshed his memory by hunting up a passage; but the patchwork process which scholarship has revealed where no ordinary reader would have suspected it, must in the main have been the work of a fine memory. It is at least easier to think he knew his favoured passages by heart than to suppose him surrounded by a sea of medieval manuscripts, fishing through them for a couplet here and an illustration there.

But had he no shame in these undivulged borrowings? On the contrary. They were matter for self-congratulation and for the gratitude of those from whom he borrowed. The notion of property in an idea is comparatively modern. It arises from the possibility of selling an idea in all available markets, and until printing was invented and became general no such possibility existed. In Chaucer's day a poem was 'published' in one of two ways, generally in both: the first was to declaim or 'sing' it (to use Chaucer's own verb for this method, given in *Troilus and Criseyde*) to an assembled company (at Court, in a private garden, in a tavern, or some such place), and the second to have it multiplied in manuscript, a slow and costly process very liable to error.

It follows that neither Froissart nor Machault nor the heirs of Guillaume de Lorris could lose a pennyworth by Chaucer's 'thefts'. And, far more important, they acquired fame by it, they became known abroad as poets. Thus, in rifling the stores of French poetry Chaucer was seeking to extend a pleasure that was by nature free. He was bringing to England, to a Court ready to appreciate it, a kind of elegance it could never have touched in isolation from Europe. The interchange was appreciated on both sides of the water. He was not stealing but propagating French culture. He had

> Semé les fleurs et planté le rosier;
> Aux ignorans de la langue pandras
> Grand translateur, noble Geoffrey Chaucier!

So sang Deschamps, sending Chaucer some poems of his own.

Chaucer to Deschamps seems no plagiary, but one who by translation is illuminating a barbarous place, one in whose garden (he modestly adds) he himself would be no more than a nettle.

And it is indeed true of *The Book of the Duchess* that its supreme poetical achievement is its courtliness, a perfect simplicity at one with a perfect sophistication. The exquisite manners that have no formality, shown between Chaucer and the Man in Black, are exactly the manners extended by Chaucer to his readers. They are at once invited into his quiet confidence. He treats them as if they were princes, and indeed as if he were a prince himself.

To whatever he describes in the poem he has a like attitude of engaged pleasure. As he seems to appreciate his reader, so he appreciates Ovid, or the little whelp . . .

> A whelp, that fauned me as I stood,
> That hadde yfolowed, and koude no good.
> Hyt com and crepte to me as lowe
> Ryght as hyt hadde me yknowe,
> Helde doun hys hed and joyned hys eres,
> And leyde al smothe doun his heres.

He enters with an exactly appropriate excitement of pleasure and perception into the forest and its game. Here the lines give a picture that has all the formality and all the freedom of manners made perfect, a style which may be seen exactly if unconsciously repeated in the loveliest of the paintings ascribed to Paolo Uccello that hangs in the Ashmolean Museum at Oxford, and is called *The Hunt at Night*.

In this picture, under a sky of deep night-blue, where there floats a feathery edge of moon, a great grove of regularly spaced and slender trees stretches into a far and dusky perspective. The slender boles are branchless until they burst forth into leafy umbrellas, high above the forest floor. Against the stillness and the darkness there is a splendid rout of riders, hounds, and servants of the hunt; men are for the most part in brightest gules; every figure has animation and a variety of stance proper to a view-holloa, somehow combined with the static formality of heraldic imagination as in other of his paintings, and as in Chaucer's poem:

The mayster-hunte [1] anoon, fot-hot,
With a gret horn blew thre mot [2]
At the uncoupylynge of hys houndes . . .
                              so at the laste
This hert rused, and staal away [3]
Fro alle the houndes a privy way.
The houndes had overshote hym alle [4] . . .

And every tree stood by hymselve
Fro other wel ten foot or twelve.
So grete trees, so huge of strengthe,
Of fourty or fifty fadme [5] lengthe,
Clene withoute bowgh or stikke,
With croppes [6] brode, and eke as thikke—
They were nat an ynche asonder—
That hit was shadewe overal under;
And many an hert and many an hynde
Was both before me and behynde. . . .

The courtliness of style that pervades this poem is
nowhere so perfect in its approach to its subject as in all
that the Man in Black has to say of his lost mistress, the
lady Blanche, and of his wooing of her. Passion and
respect, joy in her beauty, her dancing, her singing,
sorrow and longing in her loss, his service and her
surrender, all are told with an extraordinary force and
gentleness; it is the language of good breeding voicing
the thoughts and feelings of a man both natural and
civilized. In the Chaucerian conception of a gentleman
there is always something godlike mixed with something
utterly humble; there is a fine intelligence and a total
simplicity; and while it has something of the Prince in a
fairy tale, it lacks nothing of that robust actuality which

[1] Chief huntsman, hot-foot.   [2] Three notes on a horn.
[3] Roused and stole away.
[4] The hounds had all overshot him.
[5] Fathom.   [6] Tops.

Chaucer can bestow more surely than almost any other English poet.

The picture given of Blanche is Chaucer's first effort in extended portraiture, an art in which he learnt later to excel by condensation. Even though she is the subject of the poem, her description may be thought to be a little too much drawn out. Yet it is touching; her beauty and her character are well matched and so credibly presented that they hardly seem idealized or conventional, in spite of so many touches of the fashions in womanly beauty of the day.

> And every day hir beaute newed . . .

> I sawgh hyr daunce so comlily,
> Carole and synge so swetely
> Laughe and pleye so womanly . . .

> For every heër on hir heed
> Soth to seyne, hyt was not red,
> Ne nouther yelowe, ne broun hyt nas,
> Me thoghte most lyk gold hyt was.
> And whiche eyen my lady hadde!
> Debonaire, goode, glade, and sadde,[1]
> Symple, of good mochel,[2] noght to wyde . . .

> And which a goodly, softe speche
> Had that swete, my lives leche! [3]

> Hyr throte, as I have now memoyre,
> Semed a round tour of yvoyre. . . .

Conventional as this may be, it does not forbid us to believe it was a true portrait of the Duchess Blanche. Why indeed should the Duke of Lancaster not have a fashionable wife? It is hardly likely that a poet who had known

---

[1] Serious.   [2] Of fair proportion.
[3] Physician.

her and who was offering such an elegy to her widower should paint her other than she was. However that may be, the poem has a form and mood in which the interplay of dream and reality, of tradition and experiment, wandering suggestion and bright detail, show the shape of Chaucer's mind at that time, and so many of the powers and ingredients of his later poetry in this, his first large achievement as an original writer.

4
BIOGRAPHICAL (II)
(1370–1386)

CHAUCER WAS now an Esquire, a step in his advancement first recorded in 1368. As such he received sevenpence halfpenny a day and had two robes a year or forty shillings in lieu, a total well over £500 in our money. This was paid him by the old king, Edward III, in return for duties less menial than those of a valet. He had done with folding clothes, making beds, and carrying candles.

The duties laid down for an Esquire were 'Winter and Summer in afternoons and evenings, to draw to Lords' chambers within the Court, there to keep honest company after his cunning, in talking of chronicles of Kings and other policies, or in piping or harping, songings or other acts marceals till the time require of departing'.

What he may have lacked as an executive musician he made up for as an inditer of poetry. These were his background duties, his standing orders. He also became liable for more specific employments, such as foreign missions. In July 1368 he was sent on some forgotten royal business to France, with two hackneys, twenty shillings for expenses, and ten pounds in notes of exchange. Early in the following year he was abroad again, soldiering this time, probably in John of Gaunt's Picardy campaign.

What is important to note is the association with John of Gaunt. Perhaps the Duke remembered him from Hatfield days a dozen years before. Certainly from this time on Chaucer's fortunes are continuously linked with those of the House of Lancaster. It was in this year that Blanche, the Duke's first Duchess, died, and it cannot have been much later that Chaucer offered him consolation in the poem we have considered. The young Esquire had indeed taken up his duties and was bettering instruction.

In 1370 Chaucer was again abroad on the King's service from June until October, the first of a new series of continental missions. The special purposes for which he was chosen are for the most part unknown, but it was no longer as a soldier, but as a civilian emissary and negotiator that he went. He was blossoming into a man of state affairs. His private affairs were also improving; Philippa was awarded a pension of ten pounds in the following year by their steady patron, in reward for her services to Constance, his second Duchess.

The next entry in the record marks a great event in his life and poetry. On 12 November 1372 Chaucer was appointed to a Commission, in company with two citizens of Genoa, to treat with their Duke in the matter of the choice of a port in England for Genoese trade. It was his first journey to Italy. Just as his journeys to France thirteen years before had baptized him into poetry, so now this business trip to Genoa, Florence, and perhaps Padua, confirmed and strengthened him a poet. A new language and a new culture opened their enormous treasure to him, once again just when he was ripe for it. A master of the French manner, he was now ready to master the Italian. It was like a second wind to him, more sustaining than the first.

It took him some time to assimilate what Italy had to teach him, and it may be well to look forward for a

D

moment five or six years to his second visit thither, when he went to Lombardy to treat with the famous Bernabo Visconti of Milan. Chaucer was sent 'for certain matters touching the expedition of the King's war'; he was away for something over three months. These two journeys between them began the creation of his Italianate period of writing, which shows itself in gradually advancing strength after *The Book of the Duchess*. This indeed is his only longer poem that is purely French in style. Because of the uncertainties of date of his compositions, it is well not to ascribe his 'Italian period' as wholly due to his first journey there in 1372. That was a beginning of the poetical process which, but for his second journey, might never have completed itself.

There is a passage in *The Canterbury Tales* that seems to bear on his first Italian journey. The Clerk of Oxford, when asked by Harry Bailey to tell a plain story, replies:

> I wol yow telle a tale which that I
> Lerned at Padowe of a worthy clerk,
> As preved by his wordes and his werk.
> He is now deed and nayled in his cheste,
> I prey to God so yeve his soule reste!
> Fraunceys Petrak, the lauriat poete,
> Highte this clerk. . . . [1]

It was once harmlessly believed that this passage revealed an incident in Chaucer's own life on the Italian trip of 1372, but an austerer scholarship now rules this out as an improbable fancy. For all that, those who like to think Chaucer met Petrarch may do so without being absolutely convicted of error. Whether he met him or not, he came upon his expanded Latin version of the last

[1] Was the name of this learned man.

story in the *Decameron*, and turned it into *The Clerk of Oxford's Tale.*

Chaucer has another reference to 'my maister Petrak' in the story of Zenobia, one of the tragedies that, taken together, make up *The Monk's Tale.* In fifteen out of the fifty-one manuscripts of this tale there is a heading *De casibus virorum illustrium,* and this is a title borrowed from Boccaccio. A stanza of Chaucer's Zenobia is imitated from Boccaccio's treatment of the same story. From these entanglements it may perhaps be conjectured that Chaucer came upon the story of Griselda and the *De casibus* together and somehow associated them with the name of Petrarch. Perhaps Petrarch showed them to him, perhaps not. Certainly Boccaccio, whose name is never mentioned by Chaucer, was far more important to him than ever Petrarch was. Indeed he was to quarry more from him than from any other single writer, and without acknowledgement.

The style of *The Clerk's Tale* and *The Monk's Tale* would fit with the view that they were for the most part early work in the Italian vein and it is perhaps not wrong to believe that they were the chief spoils of his first Italian journey.

The voyage of 1372 started on 1 December; six months later he was back in England, evidently the expert in matters Genoese, for he was sent almost immediately to investigate some affair that had blown up about a Genoese merchant at the port of Dartmouth, a port he was later to celebrate as the home of his piratical Shipman, 'woning fer by Weste'. He was now well in the saddle of minor public affairs, and had shown himself ripe for a permanent appointment. Obviously he had been a success negotiating these Genoese matters; he was beginning to know something about foreign commerce and the complications of import, harbour dues, smuggling, and the like. All this was rewarded in 1374; on 8 June he became Comptroller of Customs and Subsidies of wools, skins, and hides at the Port of London. He was enjoined to write the rolls in his own hand and to be present at his office in person. The salary for this, augmented by an annual gift as it was, would be worth £400 or £500 a year in our money, tax-free. He was also lucky in obtaining the lease of a house rent-free in Aldgate, and the old King had ordered a pitcher of wine to be sent him every day. Presents came showering too from John of Gaunt, particularly to Philippa; six silver-gilt buttons and a silver button-hook had come as a New Year's present in 1373, and now there was a pension added of £10 a year. It was the first Italian journey that seems to have led on to these advancements. Chaucer had proved himself as a business-man; all was set for promotion.

As a Comptroller of Customs he showed efficiency and zeal. Early in the second year of his office he took charge of an action in connexion with the felonious seizure of goods; a year later he detected and confiscated a great quantity of wool which a merchant named John Kent of London had smuggled out to Dordrecht. This seems to have redounded so much to his credit that the whole value of the merchandise, namely £71 4s. 6d., was granted to Chaucer, a sum equivalent to between £2,000 and £3,000 in our day. An even greater windfall had come his way in the previous year, 1375. He was appointed guardian of two wards, which meant that he had custody over their lands and persons during their minority. One, Edward Stapelgate of Kent, aged

eighteen, paid £104 to Chaucer in respect of his ward-
ship and marriage. In these brief years he had thus
added something over £5,000 or £6,000 (in our money)
to his savings, and seemed to be laying the foundations
of an almost ministerial estate.

He was too able to be wasted in the Customs House
and was in constant demand for foreign missions. Three
times at least in 1377 he crossed the Channel on the
King's business, and was allowed to appoint a deputy
for his Comptrollership. His daily stoup of wine, for the
same reason, was commuted to a money payment.

Then came his second visit to Italy, so full of conse-
quence to English poetry. This time his chief loot was
also from Boccaccio, but on a larger scale and intrinsic-
ally finer. It consisted in the main of two works, *Il
Teseide* and *Il Filostrato*. The former was a twelve-book
epic in verse from which he was to draw descriptive
stanzas for *The Parliament of Fowls* and 'al the love of
Palamon and Arcite', mentioned in the Prologues to
The Legend of Good Women, that was later to become
The Knight's Tale. *Il Filostrato* was the story of Troilus
and Cressida as imagined by Boccaccio and was to be
transmuted into Chaucer's first full-scale masterpiece,
Troilus and Criseyde.

At some time, perhaps during his earlier visit to Italy,
Chaucer also met with the work of Dante, particularly
The Divine Comedy. The invocation at the beginning of
the Life of St. Cecilia (*The Second Nun's Tale*) is imitated
from the thirty-third Canto of the *Paradiso*, and there
are many touches in *The House of Fame*, and one in the
story of Ugolino (told by the Monk) that show Chaucer's
indebtedness to Dante, 'the grete poete of Ytaille' as he
then calls him.

There is no certainty as to the dates of Chaucer's various poems in this period. There is, however, a case for reasonable conjecture as to the extent of his output, and some agreement as to the order in which principal works came from his pen. Subject to a 'perhaps', they might be listed thus: *The Clerk's Tale*,[1] *The Second Nun's Tale*, most of *The Monk's Tale*, *The House of Fame*, *The Parliament of Fowls*, *Anelida and Arcite*, 'Palamon and Arcite', the translation of *Boethius*, and *Troilus and Criseyde*.

They seem to have been among his busiest years. He was in the prime of life, a diligent and trusted servant of the Crown, not only under the old king but also, thanks to the power of John of Gaunt, under the child Richard II who had succeeded in 1377.

After his second return from Italy little that now seems important to his poetry is recorded among his official doings until 1386. There were no more journeys abroad; he was left to settle down in his multifarious duties. That he discharged these with notable diligence can be seen from a bonus paid him in 1381 of ten marks, a present, as we should compute it, of £200 or more.[2] The uninterrupted routine of his life now gave him the chance to write, and it may not be wrong to infer from the record that his writings were beginning to receive official recognition as an activity more important than the casting of accounts and the detection of smugglers. His poetry is nowhere mentioned as such in the official records, but he won his way to obtaining permission to appoint a permanent deputy in his Comptrollership in 1384, and it may be that this was intended to allow him the leisure a poet needs.

He received another Comptrollership, this time of

[1] Less its 'Envoy'.   [2] A mark was worth 13s. 4d.

Petty Customs, in 1382; in 1385 he was associated with the Warden of the Cinque Ports as one of the Justices of the Peace for the County of Kent. On 8 August 1386 he was returned to Parliament as a Knight of the Shire for that county. But in that same year the influence of his patron, the Duke of Lancaster, was eclipsed by that of the Duke of Gloucester; Chaucer lost both his Comptrollerships, was not re-elected for Kent, and relinquished his house in Aldgate. It may be that these sacrifices were voluntary on his part; but, for whatever reason, he was never again to stand quite so prominently in public life, except as a poet. Leaving aside those works of his that were later to be included in *The Canterbury Tales*, we may now turn, at this pause in his official fortunes, to consider in their probable succession the chief poems which he had been composing against a background of state-business and court-function by day, and, by night, deep study of Virgil, Boethius, Dante, Boccaccio, and many other writers in philosophy, science, rhetoric, and poetry.[1] All this learning that in another mind might have been no more than lumber was the source and refreshment of his poetical vision

> And bathed every veyne in swich licour
> Of which vertu engendred is the flour.

---

[1] A glance at the list of authors quoted or referred to in Chaucer's poetry, as listed in Skeat's great edition, gives some idea of the extent of his reading, especially if we reflect that a writer does not necessarily quote from all the books he has read.

5

THE RING OF CANACEE

(*a*) THE HOUSE OF FAME.[1]

Perhaps it is easiest to begin with a synopsis, for in *The House of Fame* it is easy to lose one's way. Indeed, the way is uncertain and the goal never reached, for the poem, as it has come down to us, is unfinished.

Book I.—After marvelling at the inscrutable nature of dreams and suggesting many kinds and causes of them, Chaucer enters upon a poetic dream of his own, how he found himself in a Temple, wrought with great fantasy of glass; it was the Temple of Venus. There, on the walls, he found the story of her son Aeneas, painted in full from the fall of Troy to his marriage with Lavinia. His faithless treatment of Dido while at Carthage is pictured in melancholy detail, with her dying lamentation in the style of a medieval courtly lover, woefully betrayed. Meditating the nobleness of what he had seen, Chaucer, still in dream, leaves the Temple and finds himself in a wilderness. As he does so, down comes a great golden eagle out of heaven and carries off the poet into the sky 'in a swap'.

Book II.—On their airy journey, the eagle explains its purpose. Chaucer, he says, has so long celebrated lovers

[1] Scholars are not in absolute agreement as to which poem was written first, *The House of Fame* or *The Parliament of Fowls*. I have dealt with them in this order because the style of the former seems to me 'earlier'. But this opinion, even if universally entertained, would not establish its priority. A poet can go back on his work.

in his verses without receiving a lover's reward that
Jupiter has taken pity on him and ordained that he be
carried to the House of Fame, there to be given 'tidings
of love'; for every rumour on earth reaches that heavenly
house. How this can happen is then explained to the
poet—alarmed, incredulous, but passive—by the eagle,
in terms of a scientific lecture on the inherent property
in all objects to incline in certain directions, and on the
nature of sound in particular to incline towards the
House of Fame, rippling thither in waves, for a sound
is a wave of the air. The eagle offers further to explain
the stars, but Chaucer declines this kindness on the
ground that he is too old to learn. During this conversation they have been traversing heaven, away from the
dwindling earth, passing the clouds and other 'airish
beasts', and at last the dreamer is set down on a sort of
glacier below the House of Fame, and there, for a while,
the eagle leaves him.

Book III.—Chaucer scales the rocks of ice, on which
many a famous name, once carved, is thawing out, and
enters the Palace of Fame, which strikes him with
astonishment. He describes it at some length, leading
his description to a vision of Fame herself. Troop after
troop of aspirants to Fame, and some even that implore
oblivion, are seen besieging her. She answers their
petitions with unpredictable contrariety, according to
how she feels at the moment. Chaucer himself, prompted
to ask for Fame by a bystander, declines to do so, saying
he knows himself best how he stands in that regard.
He is more concerned to hear the promised tidings of
love. He is presently taken to a revolving labyrinth of
rumour made by Daedalus, where he finds his eagle once
again. As he presses forward to learn at last the love-

tidings he had come so far to hear, there suddenly appears 'a man of great authority' and, at this tantalizing moment, the poem as it has reached us is abruptly broken off.

Even if we knew how the poem ended, or was to have ended, it would be difficult to grasp this poem as an imaginative unity, for the governing idea (the quest for love-tidings) is very slenderly threaded through the maze of its subsidiary interests. The chosen form is one of a delayed surprise; the secret was only to have been revealed at the last moment in a majestic dénouement. Hints and clues are here and there embedded to stimulate the reader to a guessing kind of expectation, but unfortunately, just as the surprise is apparently to be sprung, when the *deus ex machina* is about to make all plain, the poem comes to an end in mid-sentence, and so has kept its secret for ever.

For Chaucer's courtly audience it was probably an open secret, an occasional poem of which they knew the occasion. We, however, do not; we do not even know if Chaucer finished it. He may have left it, as he left several other of his longer poems, uncompleted; or perhaps the last page or pages of his first manuscript were lost before they were copied. In either case the end is missing and it is impossible now to feel sure what 'love-tidings' were in question.

In spite of its inability to show us Chaucer's meaning as a whole, the poem has many wayside pleasures for the puzzled reader. The greatest of them lie in the Second Book, in the extraordinary conversation between the bird and the poet. This, in tone and subject, is something altogether new to English poetry, at first sight; and yet it is a sort of extension of an idea present in *The Book of the Duchess*, the discussion of a deep topic between Chaucer the Simpleton and a Wise Authority.

Indeed *The House of Fame* is patently constructed on the same general poetic scheme as the elegy for the Duchess Blanche, but more ambitiously. The main movement of each is by a dream to unfold a story of love, whose climax is held back until the end, for surprise. In each, the theme is preluded by a story from the Ancients, from Ovid and from Virgil respectively; and if we may guess a closer similarity in design, then it may be that the long tale of the betrayal of Dido by Aeneas, told in the First Book of *The House of Fame*, was chosen for narration because in some way it foreshadowed (either by likeness or contrast) the love-tidings promised by the eagle, just as the story of Ceix and Halcyon in *The Book of the Duchess* foreshadowed the loss of Blanche by the Man in Black.

The unity of mood however, so beautifully preserved throughout the earlier poem of pure elegy and lyric, is broken, book by book, in *The House of Fame*. The First Book is based in mild and serious wonder, in static description and formal narration. The Second sweeps into full comedy, leaving ancient learning for new science and centring its interest on the preposterous personal situation of a plump poet forcibly attending the disquisitions of a pedantic bird. The Third returns to a mood similar to that of the First with a description of another visionary Temple, but with more animation and ingenuity.

The unity of theme (save for the tenuous promise of 'love-tidings') is also broken. Dreams and Dido occupy the First Book, theories in physical science the Second, and the vagaries of Fame and her sister Fortune the Third. To attempt the inclusion of so many subjects, only related to each other by the ingenuity of narrative, that is, superficially, was the fundamental weakness of Chaucer's design. He was attempting too much, and in this was looking back to the old divagating, encyclopedic form of the *Roman de la Rose*. Yet he was also struggling to look forward to a newer and a more controlled way of writing. He had now read Dante, and was beginning dimly to show in his own verses the firstfruits of his reading. Not only are there individual lines taken from *The Divine Comedy*, but there is the palpable effort to organize his material something after the manner of Dante. This notion should not be pressed too close, for in all important respects the two poems are a universe apart. It would not even be justifiable to suggest that *The House of Fame* is a sort of parody or pastiche of Dante's work. But at however great a distance, it is under his influence. Even without the specific quotations Chaucer has taken from him, the likeness of certain organizing factors in both poems makes his indebtedness certain. These likenesses have often been remarked. Some of the more obvious are these. Each is in three major divisions. Each begins with an Invocation, the third invocation in both cases being an invocation to Apollo. Each insists upon an exact date of the vision, in Chaucer 10 December (though he is regrettably silent as to the year), in Dante, Good Friday 1300. There are deserts and eagles and steep rocks and lectures in both. Upon the general unwieldiness of his subject-matter (no poetical sin by the standards of Jean de Meun) Chaucer was trying to impose something of the logical shaping-power of Italian poetry. His journeys to the Dukes of Genoa and Lombardy were having their first literary result.

Incomplete, and disjunctive in mood and matter, *The House of Fame* now seems the least successful of Chaucer's longer poems. Yet it has moments of a new greatness, some of which equal anything he was to write of their kind, instance those passages of scientific exposition and visual description, and above all of personal self-revelation that flicker with a new kind of comedy. In a transitional poem such as this there are also passages less perfect, but hardly less interesting in his development; for by a comparison we can see and value his later accomplishment on the same themes, such as that of Dido.

As for us, so for Chaucer, dreams were a matter for scientific and philosophical inquiry, whether they were the dreams of poets or of lovers or of humours of the blood, dreams of the soul or belly, dreams that were no more than a rag-bag of past impressions and dreams that, being true visions of the future, had metaphysical importance since they seemed to establish that the future was in some way already fixed. This thought involves some degree of pre-destination and therefore, as Chaucer perceived, qualifies theories of the freedom of the will. It was in the *Roman de la Rose* that he had learnt the elements of this discussion, and his natural curiosity once awakened drove him to search further for an understanding of dreams. To the end of his life their fascination held; what Pertelote and Chantecleer were to say of them in later years was first adumbrated in *The House of Fame*.

God turne us every drem to goode!
For hyt is wonder, be the roode,
To my wyt, what causeth swevenes [1]
Eyther on morwes or on evenes . . .

As yf folkys complexions [2]
Make hem dreme of reflexions;
Or ellys thus, as other sayn,
For to gret feblenesse of her brayn,
By abstinence, or by seknesse. . . .
That som man is to [3] curious
In studye, or melancolyous . . .

Or yf that spirites have the myght
To make folk to dreme a-nyght . . .

Such speculations on dreams (and this part of the poem contains many more) are the ancestors to Hamlet's on the ghost, and some are surprisingly near to many of our twentieth-century notions. It is written in a tone of modest philosophical perplexity, such as may well and seriously have enveloped the poet after passing from the dream-lore of the *Roman de la Rose* to a more detailed study of Macrobius, who in commenting upon the Dream of Scipio, distinguished five kinds of dream, of which the first has five sub-divisions. It was a thorny subject.

Clearer than his questionings about the source of dreams is the opinion of the eagle concerning the laws of gravity and sound, taken by the sagacious bird from the writings of Boethius. Everything in nature has its natural resting-place, whither it strives, as the soul to

[1] Dreams.
[2] i.e. their 'humour'. Dame Pertelote adopts and expounds this view in *The Nun's Priest's Tale*. The 'colour' of a man's 'humour' (e.g. red or black) is *reflected* in the images that afflict his dreams (e.g. red dogs, black devils).
[3] Too.

God. It has a 'kyndely enclynyng' or 'natural inclina-
tion' which it must follow:

> . . . . loo, thou maist alday se
> That any thing that hevy be,
> As stoon, or led. . . .
> Lat goo thyn hand, hit falleth doun.
> Ryght so seye I be fyr or soun,
> Or smoke, or other thynges lyghte;
> Alwey they seke upward on highte.

His doctrine of sound is even more up-to-date, and
proved to Chaucer by Experience as well as by
Authority:

> Soun ys noght but eyr ybroken,
> And every speche that ys spoken,
> Lowd or pryvee, foul or fair,
> In his substaunce ys but air . . .

> I preve hyt thus—take hede now—
> Be experience; for yf that thow
> Throwe on water now a stoon,
> Wel wost thou, hyt wol make anoon
> A litel roundell as a sercle, . . .
> And ryght anoon thow shalt see wel,
> That whel wol cause another whel,[1]
> And that the thridde, and so forth, brother, . . .
> And whoso seyth of trouthe I varye,
> Bid hym proven the contrarye.
> And ryght thus every word, ywis,
> That lowd or pryvee spoken ys,
> Moveth first an ayr aboute,
> And of thys movynge, out of doute,
> Another ayr anoon ys meved,
> As I have of the watir preved. . . .

Visual descriptions offer more scope for beauty of image
than these ingenious lectures; Chaucer was to prove

[1] Wheel.

himself a master in describing palaces and temples in
The Knight's Tale and elsewhere, and here in this poem
there are two, or rather three, if to his pictures of the
Temple of Venus and the Palace of Fame we add that
of the wicker-house of Rumour, that revolves and
squeaks as it revolves.

Perhaps the most sensitive and imaginative description is of that aeronaut view of the receding earth, far
below the captive poet, as he sails upwards in the claws
of his preceptor:

> And y adoun gan loken thoo,
> And beheld feldes and playnes,
> And now hilles, and now mountaynes, . . .
> Now ryveres, now citees,
> Now tounes, and now grete trees,
> Now shippes seyllynge in the see. . . .
>
> Tho gan y loken under me
> And beheld the ayerissh bestes,[1]
> Cloudes, mystes, and tempestes,
> Snowes, hayles, reynes, wyndes,
> And th'engendrynge in hir kyndes,
> All the wey thrugh which I cam.
> 'O God!' quod y, 'that made Adam,
> Moche ys thy myght and thy noblesse!'

For one who had never been up in a balloon and who
could only have had an imaginative experience of the
tops of clouds, this description is a fine flight of power.
The surprise and beauty of the last phrase quoted packs
the couplet with that kind of joy in the created world,
in things existent for existing, which is at the base of
Chaucer's warmth, humour, and sturdiness of mind.
This joyful reaction to things created is what enables him

---

[1] Aerial creatures.

to glory in the nine spheres of heaven and the galaxy and the wart on the nose of a miller. They are things perfect in their kind and proper in their place. God be praised for them!

The House of Fame is best known, however, for what Chaucer has told us of himself in it. In the Second Book the eagle opens a window on the poet's private life, so that we catch a mocking glimpse of Philippa Chaucer herself.

> 'Awak', to me he seyde,
> Ryght in the same vois and stevene [1]
> That useth oon I koude nevene [2] ...

Philippa, as we know, was a lady in waiting on the Queen, and therefore may well be supposed to have been present at the reading of this poem to the Court. Even if it was never finished and therefore never read, it would have been written with the intention of that kind of publication. The gibe, therefore, at the way in which his wife used to wake him in the morning seems an affectionate one, matter for a titter in his audience rather than a suggestion of serious domestic unhappiness. The views Chaucer chose later to express on marriage, particularly in the Wife of Bath's preamble, may represent his settled opinion reached many years after Philippa's death. On the other hand, since these are a tissue of the opinions of St. Jerome, Walter Map, Eustache Deschamps, and Jean de Meun, they may represent no more than an amusing and traditional attitude, appropriate to the Wife herself. How Geoffrey got on with Philippa remains their own secret.

The eagle also comments on Chaucer's own life,

---

[1] Tone.   [2] Name.

making him out a mild, unsociable hermit, given to
drowsing and browsing over books:

> But of thy verray neyghebores,
> That duellen almost at thy dores,
> Thou herist [1] neyther that ne this;
> For when thy labour doon al ys,
> And hast mad alle thy rekenynges,
> In stede of reste and newe thynges,
> Thou goost hom to thy hous annon,
> And, also domb as any stoon,
> Thou sittest at another book
> Tyl fully daswed [2] is thy look. . . .

The hen-pecked husband, the weary Customs official and
the student of ancient philosophy and Italian poets, home
in his house in Aldgate, suddenly thrust their solid way
among these airy fantasies.

These best things in the poem are much above the
reach of *The Book of the Duchess*; they must also have been
more difficult to write, a criterion Dryden allows in
judging poetry. As unity was the triumph of that poem,
so diversity of interest is the triumph of this.

In some ways he still had much to teach himself, most
of all, perhaps, in versification. *The House of Fame* is in
the beginner's metre of the eight-syllabled couplet that
halts the flow of invention, and, as in Gower, seems to
leave little room in a line for anything but bare narrative. It is a stumbling metre, too, insecure in its disposition of stress. A fair comparison of his powers in this
early poem in his Italian period can be made by placing
his account of Aeneas and of Dido beside another he
was to write later, in the last poem he made before
turning to *The Canterbury Tales*, namely *The Legend of
Good Women*.

---

[1] Hearest.   [2] Dazed.

Here is all that is said in *The House of Fame* of the wooing and winning of Dido. It is laid briefly at the door
of Venus, who

> . . . made Eneas so in grace
> Of Dido, quene of that contree,
> That, shortly for to tellen, she
> Becam hys love, and let him doo
> Al that weddynge longeth too.[1]

There is more dignity in the measured tread of the
ten-syllable line, and the more florid manner of his later
way of writing in the *Legend*:

> This noble queen, that cleped was Dido, . . .
> That fayrer was than is the bryghte sonne,
> This noble toun of Cartage hath bigonne;
> In which she regneth in so gret honour,
> That she was holden of alle queenes flour,
> Of gentillesse, of fredom, of beaute;
> That wel was hym that myghte hire ones se; [2]
> Of kynges and of lordes so desyred,
> That al the world hire beaute hadde yfyred [3] . . .

Such as it is, however, *The House of Fame* could have
been written by no other poet than Chaucer, and even he
could not have written it if he had never been sent on
those Italian journeys.

(*b*) THE PARLIAMENT OF FOWLS

The structure of this fantasy, so much more at unity
with itself than *The House of Fame*, will easily emerge
from a synopsis.

Reading, as ever, Chaucer tells us he came upon a
book called the *Somnium Scipionis*, and after giving a

---

[1] All that belongs to wedding.
[2] That it was well for him who might see her, even once.
[3] That her beauty had fired all the world.

brief account of what is in it, he describes how night fell and he went to bed, and in a dream this Scipio appeared to him, and took him into a walled garden. There are many kinds of tree there, a host of flowers, a charm of birds, music, and a temperate air. He sees Cupid and Venus and Priapus, Beauty, Flattery, Foolhardiness and all the abstractions proper to such a garden, and lastly the noble goddess Nature herself. It is St. Valentine's Day, and she has summoned the birds in their hierarchies before her, from the royal tercel eagle to the cock that is the clock of little towns, and lower still, to goose and cuckoo, to decide on which shall win for his love the formel eagle on her wrist. Three eagles, one after another, state their claim and plead to be rewarded, and a free-for-all argument ensues. Each group of birds chooses a spokesman, and each spokesman puts a point of view suited to the nobleness or scurrility of his kind. The goose, for the water-fowl, says that if a lover be refused by one let him choose another. The turtle, for the seed-fowl, says God forbid that a lover should ever change his choice; in which opinion the duck can find neither reason nor wit. The cuckoo, for the worm-fowl, says that so long as he gets a mate, he does not care who goes without. The goddess of Nature decides the debate by leaving the formel to choose for herself, though she advises her to choose the royal tercel, because of his royalty. The formel eagle asks for a year's respite. This is granted and Nature dismisses the assembly after putting the three eagle-aspirants on a year's probation. All birds join in a carol in honour of St. Valentine, and Chaucer awakes and turns to his books again.

However perfectly accomplished, a poem about an assembly of birds debating courtly love may well be passed over as trivial, one of the toys of poetry made to give a passing pleasure and no more. When its perfect workmanship of language and its luxurious imagery have caught our attention, we may feel it a pity that so much art should have been squandered on so light a subject.

Yet although he intended it as a playful poem, a frolic for St. Valentine's Day, he had chosen for his playground our serious universe as it was then conceived. Beneath the fashions and the feathers there lies a settled faith and vision of reality, not to be judged by the question whether birds can talk or argue love after the fashion of the Court. Nor is it even a question of allegorical interpretation. The sense of seriousness and wide-eyed truth to nature that he conveys does not depend on our reading Richard II for the royal tercel and Anne of Bohemia for the formel eagle. These may indeed have been intended by the poet, or, if not, some other persons of his acquaintance at that time. But the substitution of historical figures for birds will not add much to our understanding why this poem is a masterpiece, or what kind of masterpiece it is.

The vision from which *The Parliament of Fowls* draws all its strength is of two aspects of reality clearly and universally seen in Chaucer's day, namely the noble hierarchies of The Natural Order under God and of the social gradations in feeling and delicacy in sexual love. In this poem Chaucer has made a harmony of these two hierarchies, from which the other beauties of diction and imagery spring. Fancy can use them freely for a playground and be safe, for out of such a vision there can come a frivolity, but it is secured from what is trivial or facetious. Or if we say the poem is purely decorative, the decoration follows a structural line. Chaucer was using decoration, but he knew the shape of the whole building, and so did his first audience. It was the shape of their universe and of their code.

It begins, as *The Book of the Duchess* and *The House of Fame* began, with a classical text, this time from Cicero, the *Somnium Scipionis*, to which Macrobius had added a commentary. As before, Chaucer gives a paraphrase of his author, recording how the young Scipio is taken by his ancestor, Scipio Africanus, to 'a starry place', and there is told that

> . . . oure present worldes lyves space
> Nis but a maner deth,[1] what wey we trace,[2]
> And rightful folk shul gon, after they dye,
> To hevene; and shewed hym the Galaxye.
>
> Thanne shewede he hym the lytel erthe that here is,
> At regard of the hevenes quantite;
> And after shewede he hym the nyne speres,[3] . . .

Pondering this book after night has fallen, Chaucer goes to bed and falls into the expected dream; Africanus appears to him fresh from his vision of the universe, and takes him to such a garden as we have seen in the *Roman de la Rose*, peopled by the abstractions of love, and by their gods and goddesses, under the supremacy of Nature.

> Tho was I war wher that ther sat a queene
> That, as of lyght the somer sonne shene
> Passeth the sterre, right so over mesure
> She fayrer was than any creature.
>
> And in a launde, upon an hil of floures,
> Was set this noble goddesse Nature.

---

[1] A kind of death.   [2] Whatever way we take.
[3] Spheres.

And that we may not mistake her power and quality, her harmonious command of the elements, and her authority over living creatures, she is described as sorting out the birds before her for the ordering of their yearly mating:

> This noble emperesse, ful of grace,
> Bad every foul to take his owne place,
> As they were woned [1] alwey fro yer to yeere,
> Seynt Valentynes day, to stonden theere. . . .

> Nature, the vicaire of the almyghty Lord,
> That hot, cold, hevy, lyght, moÿst, and dreye
> Hath knyt by evene noumbres of acord, [2]
> In esy voys began to speke and seye,
> 'Foules, tak hed of my sentence, I preye. . . .'

This is the setting for the fantasy, which arises from a full and steady gaze upon reality as it was known to Chaucer. So, in the debate which follows, he looks steadily at the idea of love, how it is differently desired by different kinds of creature. The desire of the male for the female in the noblest rises above appetite into service, which, to the less noble, is foolishness. Yet this ideal of love survives a realist mockery, inasmuch as the mockers do not understand the thing they are mocking; the goose and duck, glowing with common sense, unwittingly write themselves down no more than ducks or geese.

> Al this nys not worth a flye!

is the latter's comment on the aristocratic declarations of the Tercel eagles. The nobler sparrow-hawk rebukes her:

> 'Lo, here a parfit resoun of a goos!'

---

[1] Accustomed.
[2] That has knit in even and harmonious number the qualities of heat, cold, heaviness, lightness, moisture and dryness.

Every bird that speaks puts its own point of view, appropriate to its rank in nature and therefore to its grasp on what is proper to love. Years later, in *The Canterbury Tales*, Chaucer was to show the same variety of approach to the relations of male and female in a world of human beings.

Just as *The Parliament of Fowls* is a harmony of serious vision and light fancy, so it is one of the older French and newer Italian traditions. The dream of an allegorical garden and a love-debate were from the French style of poem, but the new luxury of colouring is Italian. Chaucer took a hint once more from Dante, this time in framing the inscriptions over the gateways of his garden, imitated, at a distance from the famous

Lasciate ogni speranza voi ch'entrate.

But he was beginning to find that Boccaccio, not Dante, was his real blood-brother in authorship, and in this poem is found one of the first of his copious transfusions. Many stanzas are taken and imitated from the *Teseide*, of which this may serve as an example. It describes the goddess Venus:

> Hyre gilte heres with a golden thred
> Ibounden were, untressed as she lay,
> And naked from the brest unto the hed
> Men myghte hire sen; and, sothly for to say,
> The remenaunt was wel kevered to my pay.[1]
> Ryght with a subtyl coverchef of Valence—
> Ther nas no thikkere cloth of no defense.

It is hardly enough to say this is Italian in origin; it is Italian in feeling too. Just as in *The Book of the Duchess* there were foretastes of the painting of Uccello displayed

[1] To my taste.

by Chaucer even before he had touched the shores of Italy, so here, in *The Parliament of Fowls*, there are fore-tastes of such as Botticelli and Bronzino, almost of Titian or Tintoretto. Chaucer's visit to Italy had launched him securely into the main stream of European tradition and he has caught a manner at once retrospective and prophetic, even if these painters, whose flavour of re-naissance luxury he was the first to capture, did not know his work. But doubtless they knew Boccaccio, and drew from him and an Italian sun as Chaucer did.

In this poem Chaucer has found room for the thoughts that haunt all his other work; his preoccupation with dreams, his sense of his own spectatorship at the feast of human love, his faculties of conversation. The theories that account for dreams, which he had set down with a show of modest perplexity in *The House of Fame*, now resolve themselves into a theory that a man's habitual occupation dictates his dreams:

> The wery huntere, slepynge in his bed,
> To wode ayeyn his mynde goth anon;
> The juge dremeth how his plees been sped;
> The cartere dremeth how his cartes gon . . .

This was a theory Shakespeare was to steal, or share, and place in the mouth of Mercutio:

> And in this state she gallops night by night
> Through lovers' brains, and then they dream of love;
> O'er courtiers' knees, that dream on courtesies,
> O'er lawyers' fingers, who straight dream on fees;
> O'er ladies' lips, who straight on kisses dream. . . .

As we have learnt from his earlier poems to expect, Chaucer is treated by his visionary instructor with affable contempt. Scipio rubs in, what the eagle had already told him, that love is not a thing for such as Chaucer to

enjoy; it is enough that he may watch it in others (like
his own Pandarus, somewhat volatilized), and to make
what poetry he can out of that:

> 'But natheles, although that thow be dul,
> Yit that thow canst not do, yit mayst thow se,
> For many a man that may nat stonde a pul,
> It liketh hym at the wrastlyng for to be,
> And demeth yit wher he do bet or he.
> And if thow haddest connyng for t'endite,
> I shal the [1] shewe mater of to wryte.'

In love, in dreams, in the wide vision of nature and
in the mocking knowledge of himself Chaucer's art had
steadily deepened as his understanding enriched itself in
France and Italy. The progress of these themes from *The
Book of the Duchess* to *The Parliament of Fowls*, cast as they
are in allegory, is the measure of his own progress towards
that poetry of people he was so soon to write without
parable, and in which his skill in conversation was to
play so large a part. That skill itself had greatly developed. The eagle in *The House of Fame* talked better
than the Man in Black; and now, in *The Parliament of
Fowls*, the very ducks talk better than the eagle

> 'Wel bourded,' quod the doke, 'by myn hat! [2]
> That men shulde loven alwey causeles,
> Who can a resoun fynde or wit in that? . . .
> Ye quek!' yit seyde the doke, ful wel and fayre,
> 'There been mo sterres, God wot, than a payre!' [3]

When it comes to the language of birds, Chaucer
seems to have had the magic ring of Canacee.[4] Yet even

---

[1] Thee.
[2] 'My hat, that's a good joke!' said the duck.
[3] 'God knows, there are more stars than a pair.'
[4] In *The Squire's Tale* Canacee is possessed of a ring which
enables her to understand bird-language.

these, his earlier birds, were not so idiomatic as Chanticleer and Pertelote, still to be created.

Chaucer was shaking free also of the octosyllabic
metre, which hardly any but the extreme genius of
Milton, and of Chaucer himself, can use in serious poetry
without a jingle or a jog-trot. Even in Chaucer it is
often limiting and unsatisfactory. He was entering upon
a period of stanzaic poetry, the disciplined power of
the ten-syllabled line and the interweaving of rhymes, a
kind of poetry suited to a greater reach of thought, a
more serious narration. Twenty-five per cent. extra in
metrical length allows a line to carry more than that in
added meaning and majesty.

The stanza form he found, or could have found in
France. Machault had already written in what we call
'rhyme royal',[1] the metre of *The Parliament of Fowls*, the
metre-to-be of *Troilus and Criseyde*.

The Parliament of Fowls is the most perfectly imagined
and contrived of all his poems up to that date, and there
is only one respect in which it may be felt to fall short of
his earlier performances: it is a little deficient in intimacy.
The feelings evoked for the royal tercel and his mate
have no poignancy, as have those we feel for the Man in
Black in *The Book of the Duchess*, and the warmth lent to
The House of Fame by Chaucer's personal colloquies with
the eagle is absent from *The Parliament of Fowls*, for he
does not use his own presence in the poem so richly.
There is a glimpse or two at the beginning:

The lyf so short, the craft so long to lerne, *et seq.*

---

[1] So called from its use in *The Kyngis Quair*, a fifteenth-
century poem attributed to King James of Scotland.

and at the end:

> And with the shoutyng, whan the song was do [1]
> That foules maden at here flyght awey,
> I wok, and other bokes tok me to
> To reede upon, and yit I rede alwey. . . .

But for the rest he is little more than an observant spectator, as he was so soon to be again in *Troilus and Criseyde*.

At the end of the *Parliament*, as in *The Book of the Duchess*, the poet circled back to his opening thought, the thought of a book of ancient authority, and so the shape of both poems is that of a boomerang journey out and back in a wide and graceful ring. Perhaps *The House of Fame*, were it complete, would show the same pattern. It was time he found another formula if his art as a writer was to develop. It was in Boethius that he found one, the formula of the Turn of Fortune's Wheel, the formula for Tragedy. It was a new kind of circle. With a sudden release of imaginative strength Chaucer burst out of his earlier ring-form and made his first entry into the realm of major poetry.

[1] Done.

6

'HIGH SERIOUSNESS'

'Fable or Allegory are a totally distinct and **inferior** kind of Poetry. Vision or Imagination is a Representation of what Eternally exists, Really and Unchangeably . . . Note here that Fable or Allegory is seldom without some vision. Pilgrim's Progress is full of it, the Greek poets the same; but Allegory and Vision ought to be known as two Distinct Things, and so call'd for the sake of Eternal Life.'

William Blake: *A Vision of the Last Judgement* (1810)

JUDGED BY the standards of William Blake, Chaucer was moving steadily from a lesser mode of poetry towards the poetry of vision. *The Book of the Duchess, The House of Fame,* and *The Parliament of Fowls* are 'seldom without some vision', and I have tried to trace in them the things that make for a changeless poetry in the midst of bygone fashions in decoration.

A reader of *Troilus and Criseyde* might think himself to be still in an old-time tapestry tale (shorn, however, of formal allegory), until the first entry of Pandarus. From that moment we are in the modern world of the interplay of character. Pandarus is Chaucer's first creation of a piece of actuality with no model before him but life itself. Pandarus is the first grown-up in English, the first worldling, the first figure of *Canterbury Tales* dimension. He is a match for the Wife of Bath. His round and complicated personality bubbles suddenly out of the archaic romance like new wine out of an old bottle. He is on a Shakespearian scale, being for many things a sort of blend of Falstaff and Polonius, nearer the latter for his busy stratagems and platitudes, nearer the former for his elderly impishness and his deep and almost sensual affection for his Prince. Like Falstaff, too, he is never at a loss, equal to any occasion except the supreme occasion. For he is as useless and pathetic at the end as Falstaff in his rejection.

A diligent eye may see in the plumage of Pandarus some duck and goose feathers from *The Parliament of Fowls*, perhaps even an eagle feather from *The House of Fame*. In these briefer exhibitions of comic power we may see unconscious preliminary sketches. Pandarus himself, however, is fully fledged.

That the central figure in a tragedy of young love should be an elderly comedian is a stroke of unique originality in Chaucer. Tragi-comedy is a kind of vision we associate most readily with the genius of Shakespeare, but it was Chaucer who discovered it. It is a kind of writing in which a hidden philosophic seriousness underlies the smiling account of human behaviour, the tears and the buffoonery, and gives them a secret direction. Only at the end of the journey do we realize where we have been taken.

But at first sight this secret philosophical trend is hardly perceptible, for the more manifest human interest captivates us so strongly. We find ourselves reading what seems a rather gay psychological novel with a modern texture of idiomatic conversation and a well-observed detail of daily incident, the whole charged with humour, tenderness, and a poetical feeling for actuality. So we are led to feel the poem on the personal plane alone, as if it were no more than the sad story of two lovers, one inconstant, and their go-between, in the

familiar setting of courtly love. As we read on we learn
with pity that Criseyde was false, and if we restrict our
attention to the personal plane, the poem seems a compassionate study of the faint-hearted fickleness of a girl,
or perhaps of girls in general. But it is much more than
that, and Chaucer has expressly warned us against
resting in this thought.[1] He was not concerned to show
the falseness of women but the falseness of courtly love
itself.

To perceive this it is first necessary to grasp the form
in which the poem is cast. Chaucer calls it a tragedy.
It is the first tragedy consciously conceived as such in
English. Tragedy has acquired so many forms, most of
them discerned by Shakespeare, that when we speak
loosely of a tragedy, we scarcely mean more than a story
of exceptional calamity. To Chaucer 'tragedy' had a
preciser meaning. It was a story of specific shape, a shape
laid down for him by Boethius, in the Second Book of
his *Consolation of Philosophy*. Chaucer's own translation
of the essential passage reads thus:

'What other thyng bywaylen the cryinges of tragedyes
but oonly the dedes of Fortune, that with unwar strook
overturneth the realmes of greet nobleye?'[2]

To which he added a gloss of his own:

'*Tragedye is to seyn a dite of prosperite for a tyme, that
endith in wrecchidnesse.*'

Many times he came back in thought to this passage.
It underlies the whole conception of *Troilus and
Criseyde*. It was a doctrine with which he had already

[1] e.g. in Book V, lines 1772–78.
[2] What else do the lamentings of tragedies bewail, save only
the deeds of Fortune, which with an unpredictable stroke
overturn kingdoms of great majesty. *Comment: Tragedy
means a ditty of prosperity for a time that ends in wretchedness.*

experimented in his *De casibus virorum illustrium* that was
later to become *The Monk's Tale*:

> I wol biwaille, in manere of tragedie,
> The harm of hem that stoode in heigh degree,
> And fillen [1] so that ther nas no remedie
> To brynge hem out of hir adversitee.
> For certein, whan that Fortune list to flee,
> Ther may no man the cours of hire with-holde . . .

and, at the conclusion,

> Tragediës noon oother maner thyng
> Ne kan in syngyng crie ne biwaile [2]
> But that Fortune alwey wole assaile
> With unwar strook the regnes that been proude;
> For whan men trusteth hire, thanne wol she faille,
> And covere hire brighte face with a clowde.

All is Fortune, as Malvolio was to say. She casts a man
down from bliss and power to a miserable end, unavoid-
able and irremediable. It is the element of ill luck in
life that seems, in special cases, to be so paramount as
only to be explainable in terms of some universal, hostile
power. That was the shape of Chaucer's new kind of
poem.

It was also to be the shape of Shakespeare's first
tragedy, written in the Chaucerian years of *Richard II*
and *A Midsummer Night's Dream*, the tragedy of *Romeo
and Juliet*. These lovers, like Troilus and Criseyde, also
have for their go-between a figure of comedy that carries
its own kind of damnation within it; the Nurse and
Pandar are not far apart. Romeo and Juliet are also

---

[1] Fell.

[2] Tragedies can lament nothing in their song but that
Fortune &c.

lovers crossed by a hostile universe. Even before meeting Juliet, Romeo had some premonition of that

> Some consequence, yet hanging in the stars
> Shall bitterly begin his fearful date
> With this night's revels;

This conception must cast a philosophical as well as a poetical colouring over any poem built out of it. For unless the notion of Fortune is used as a thoughtless fancy, it must involve some denial of free will.

Whether or not our wills are free was a question never far from Chaucer's mind after he had read Boethius. It was linked not only with the fiction of the goddess Fortune but also with his interest in dreams. Dreams were no fiction. Too many dreams of a prophetic nature had been recorded to dismiss the notion that a fatal future can sometimes be foreseen in them. And if the future can at all be foreseen, where is our free will?

Boethius, in the last Book of his *Consolation of Philosophy*, went deeply into the problem of the freedom of the will, and Chaucer saw at once how relevant the discussion was to the story of Troilus. When the stroke of destiny parted him from Criseyde, the young man perceived with anguish mounting to despair that there was nothing he could do, nothing he could have done to prevent or remedy it.

Thus *Troilus and Criseyde* is a Boethian book. But the story itself is from Boccaccio's *Il Filostrato*. One might say, using fourteenth-century terminology, that Chaucer saw in Boccaccio's tale of Troilus an *exemplum* of the Boethian philosophies of tragedy and free will, save that where Boethius finally allows us to believe that we have a measure of freedom, Troilus concludes that he has none.

F

It is only after his death that he begins to see his own tragedy in another perspective.

Il Filostrato is a strong story told without philosophical implications. Boccaccio had inherited the makings of it from the Troy Legend as he found it in Guido delle Colonne, who in turn got it from a French poet of the twelfth century, Benoit de Saint-Maure, who seems to have invented it out of scraps of information to be found in the writings of two supposed eye-witnesses of the Trojan war, Dares the Phrygian and Dictys the Cretan. Their authenticity is now generally disbelieved.

The originality of Boccaccio lay in his concentrating on the loves of Troilus and Criseyde before their separation, which in Benoit was no more than an episode in the Trojan war. Boccaccio created this type-story of a lover who wins a girl and loses her because she proves faithless, and he used it lyrically, that is, to figure forth his own personal sorrows in the loss of the faithless mistress, to whom his poem is dedicated. She may learn by it what he has suffered and is suffering on her account.

In *Il Filostrato* there are four main characters, Troilo, Criseida (sometimes spelt Griseida), Pandaro, and Diomede. These are also the main characters in Chaucer's poem, but he has greatly changed the first three. The interest of studying a source is not simply to trace the history of an idea, still less to imply any plagiarism or barrenness of invention in the later poem. It is to divine what an author saw in his original and what he saw beyond it.

By what he chooses to retain, and still more by what he chooses to alter, we can learn the drift of his mind, the shape of his intuitions, and so identify ourselves with his intention. It is not always so easy to state as it is to feel the direction and quality of any changes made, but they must weight our whole understanding of any given work, where such tracings of source are possible.

The changes made by Chaucer in his handling of *Il Filostrato* are very revealing. Indeed I doubt if his final intention in writing *Troilus and Criseyde* can be known without studying them.

What he retained, namely the main line of the story, was, as I have suggested, an *exemplum* or instance of Boethian tragedy, of the turning of Fortune's wheel. It gave him a new kind of story, the story of an actuality, not of a dream. What he changed were the characters of Troilo, Criseida, and Pandaro, and through these changes fashioned his philosophical criticism not of them but of the code of love that bound them.

The nature of these changes of character and their effect on Chaucer's poem are for once easy to state. As Mr. C. S. Lewis has said, Chaucer 'medievalized them'. We must distinguish between primary and consequent changes. The primary changes are in the characters of Troilus and Criseyde; the consequent changes are in the character of Pandarus and in the detail of the narrative.

Troilus and Criseyde are 'medievalized' in the sense that they are made exactly to conform to the character and rules for the behaviour of ideal lovers as laid down in the *Roman de la Rose*. Troilo into Troilus is a less radical change than Criseida into Criseyde. Yet even his character was profoundly modified by Chaucer. It was modified towards a greater gentleness and sensibility. He is far humbler to his lady, putting her least wish above his own desires, unable to think she should look down so low as to a wretch like him. He is abashed by his own demerits, by his own temerity in venturing to offer to love. Boccaccio's hero is more for self than service, and for that reason, more what we might call 'a proper man', a little like the 'sudden' Diomede himself. Both Troilus and Troilo refuse food, lose sleep, poetize, and weep tears, for both are conventionally minded and fall in love by the book. But in every case Troilus is closer to the book than Troilo, and the book is the *Roman de la Rose*, where Cupid commands his servant to be

> As man abasshed wonder sore,
> And after syghen more and more.[1]

Even when Troilus knows himself to be accepted as a lover (though Criseyde's love to him is not yet fully accorded), he maintains a lovely humility towards her, in which he is closer to the religion of love than ever Troilo was:

> This Troilus ful soone on knees hym sette
> Ful sobrely, right be hyre beddes hed,
> And in his beste wyse his lady grette. . . .

Boccaccio's boy at that moment in the story has more dash and possessiveness:

'And to her Troilus said: "Fair lady, sole hope and bliss of my mind, ever before me has been the star of thy lovely face in its splendour and brightness; . . . it needs not to ask pardon for this."

Then he embraced her, and they kissed each other on the mouth.' (*Trans.* R. K. Gordon)

The English Troilus has not the same point-blank sexuality; he pays an almost religious homage to

---

[1] (Lovers breaking for a moment from their trance, return to consciousness of themselves) as a man sorely abashed, and then they sigh all the more.

Criseyde, which Pandarus is amused to observe and make fun of:

> But Pandarus, that so wel koude feele
> In every thyng, to pleye anon bigan,
> And seyde, 'Nece, se how this lord kan knele!
> Now, for youre trouthe, se this gentil man!'
> And with that word he for a quysshen [1] ran. . . .

So little are the thoughts of Troilus on the pleasures nearly in his grasp, so much is he, even at that last moment, still her servant, that on seeing her weep, he felt

> The crampe of deth, to streyne hym by the herte . . .
> And down he fel al sodeynly a-swowne.

This emotion, excessive in the eyes of the twentieth century perhaps, is not to be found in Boccaccio either. Chaucer has given Troilus a delicacy more proper to the allegorical gardens of de Lorris than to the world of actuality. He is a paragon of courtly love.

In presenting the character of Criseyde, Chaucer has subtilized once more. The Italian girl was easier of access, in passion unhesitant, one who makes a show of modesty for form's sake, but has no real reluctance to be loved. She can take independent action towards what is almost as much her goal as her lover's, and needs no more than minimum persuasion from Pandaro.

But Chaucer makes Criseyde a creature of reticences and reluctances; the world and its tongue alarm her. She would like to remain in an undisturbed widowhood (both authors agree as to her being a widow) for she is timid, frightened by the sieges of Troy and of herself, frightened of the Greeks, frightened of wicked tongues, fenced like the Rose in the Garden of the Rose, and with

[1] Cushion.

as little power to move of her own towards her lover as a
rose upon its stalk. But with all this retreatingness, she
is inwardly drawn by his handsome mien; to see him
ride by is a love-potion to her:

'Who yaf me drynke ?' [1]

And when at last she lies in her lover's arms and he pleads
with her to yield, she says with wonderful simpleness that
had she not inwardly yielded to him long before, she
would not now be where she was. That she loves him,
then, is certain, however much she is a holder-back.
Had it not been for another quality, namely the generous
compassion called Pitee, she would have held back longer,
perhaps entirely. But the grief of Troilus awakens pity
in her, Pitee, standard grace in the Beloved, that takes
the lover's part.

> Wommen wel ought pite to take
> Of hem that sorwen for her sake
> (*Roman de la Rose*)

and indeed we can now see the motivation of the poem
taking some shape, for if pity is so great a quality in a girl
worthy to be loved, then the lamentations of her fainting
lover have more place in the poem. The need he has
for pity is proportionate to her impulses to bestow it.

There is another thing to be said about Criseyde.
Although she fits the formula for a courtly lover she has
overtones which Troilus has not. She remains to the
end partly an enigma. One is never quite certain
whether what she says and does springs from calculation
or from impulse, and this is one of the secrets of her
attractive femininity. 'She is like an orange pip on a

[1] Who gave me to drink?

plate', as Robert Frost once said to me of another elusive creature.

Thus Chaucer has altered his hero and heroine from the bolder spirits they seem to be in Boccaccio, to creatures more conventional and of greater delicacy. We may say, if we like, that these are national differences; the passion of the South and the sentiment of the North dictate them respectively. But the true home of the Chaucerian pair is not England so much as France; he has acclimatized them to a book of rules, and, as always with Chaucer when he is drawing upon a book for his material, he seems like one drawing immediately from life.

The change in Pandarus is the most obvious and enchanting. Boccaccio invented him as a person in the story, but spent no pains on his character, leaving him hardly more than a piece of narrative machinery, a rather dull young man with cynical ideas about women and a certain energy in his wish to help Troilus his friend; there are no subtleties in him, he has no charm. Chaucer elevated Pandarus from a young cousin of Criseyde's to an uncle of uncertain age. He is a joker, full of proverbial conversation, a most dexterous manager of dinner-parties, a man of resource and invention. As a lover he has been personally so little successful as to be able to make a jest of it, but he has a cunning tact in handling the loves of his niece and Troilus. This he does out of pure good will, a good will, however, that is faintly salacious; this he feels to be so himself and therefore tries to deny it. He would like to see the young people happy and he believes he knows how to make them so. But for the stroke of Fate he would have succeeded, and for a time he did succeed. Thunderstorms he might foresee, but not Fate. In all this he seems to offer a speaking portrait of his own creator, Geoffrey Chaucer, who was in the middle forties at the time of his creation, a man of proverbs, a diplomat *de carrière*, 'a popet in an arm t'enbrace for any womman, smal and fair of face', a considerable astronomer, a man of sophistication and humour, and, above all, of kindly feeling. Perhaps this partial self-portraiture was entirely unconscious, but it is striking and may well be a reason why Pandarus is so lively and lovable. Whether or not, he is more elaborately altered from the Pandaro of Boccaccio than are any of the other figures.

If our previous analysis is true, the alteration is not primary, but consequent upon the alterations in Criseyde and Troilus. Given, in the boy, his bashfulness and humility of service and the unselfishness of his love, given, in the girl, her reluctances and fears, the off-hand methods of Boccaccio's Pandaro would never have brought the two to bed. To do this, a subtler, more authoritative character had to be created, a Pandarus older and to be leant upon, capable of sober counsel, quizzical mockery, deep affection, and wisdom of the world, somehow trustworthy, though quick as lightning in fibs and stratagems.

Such then were the main changes Chaucer made in the characters of his poem, and these changes necessitated changes in the conduct of the narrative and brought forth a new and wonderful invention of episodes consequent upon them. The most striking are the dinner-party at the house of Deiphebus and that night of thunderstorm in which, at long last, the lovers find their full joys.

In both these episodes, Pandarus is the presiding

genius. In the former his problem was to bring the bashful lovers to a first meeting, and yet arouse no suspicion in any breast, not even in Criseyde who is all innocent of the plan.

Troilus had besought Pandarus to arrange a meeting with Criseyde, and Pandarus had rejoined:

'Now lat m'alone, and werken as I may . . .'

He works to good purpose. Gathering all his powers of intrigue and improvization, he seeks out Deiphebus, the favourite brother of Troilus, and explains to him that a wretch named Poliphete is persecuting his niece, Criseyde. Deiphebus swallows this fib whole and also the suggestion delicately put forward by Pandarus that perhaps a little party of notables, invited to meet Criseyde at his house—his brothers, for instance—might lend her countenance in this persecution. The party is arranged, Paris and Helen and Hector are to be invited, and Troilus, too, a happy after-thought. Pandar's next visit is to Criseyde. Having appealed to nobleness in Deiphebus, he now appeals to timidity in her; he was a good psychologist.

> He seide, 'O verray God, so have I ronne! . . .
> Be ye naught war how false Poliphete
> Is now aboute eftsones for to plete,
> And brynge on yow advocacies newe?' [1]
> 'I? no,' quod she, and chaunged al hire hewe.

Troilus is the next to be tackled; the cock-and-bull story about Poliphete is dropped. Troilus is told about the party and how it will be a first opportunity for him to speak with Criseyde; but he must remember to feign

---

[1] Is setting immediately to work to bring a suit at law and trouble you with fresh indictments.

sick on arrival, so that he may be given a room apart.
Troilus needs no persuasion; no feigning is needed, love
has laid him low enough:

> 'For I am sik in ernest, douteles,
>   So that wel neigh I sterve for the peyne.'

So the party is assembled, the guests arrive. Troilus
'falls sick' and is taken to another room to bed, followed
by the sympathy of all concerned, none of whom suspects
a stratagem. Only God and Pandar knew.

> But [1] God and Pandare wist al what this mente.

Dinner is served, after which Pandarus makes a little
speech on the matter that has brought them together:

> 'My lordes and my ladys, it stant thus:
> What sholde I lenger,' quod he, 'do yow dwelle?'
> He rong hem out a proces [2] lik a belle
> Upon hire foo, that highte Poliphete,
> So heynous, that men myghte on it spete.[3]

It has the desired effect, and Helen, in her indignation,
suggests that perhaps Troilus could be induced to take
Criseyde's part, little knowing what she is saying.
Pandarus agrees, but stipulates that as his room is very
small, it would be better for Troilus, not to increase his
fever, if only one or two should go in to visit him.
Criseyde must go, of course, to urge her case against
Poliphete, and he himself perhaps:

> 'But wel ye woot, the chaumbre is but lite,[4]
>   And fewe folk may lightly make it warm. . . .'

This little stratagem, however, is unsuccessful, so Pandarus, with fresh resource, produces a letter from Hector
(who had not come to the party after all), and persuades

---

[1] Only.   [2] An indictment.   [3] Spit.   [4] Small.

Helen and Deiphebus to go and read it in the garden.
Pandarus has now set the stage for the meeting of Troilus
and Criseyde, and bids her visit him with Antigone, but
at the last moment turns Antigone away from the door
of the sick-room.

> Al innocent of Pandarus entente,
> Quod tho Criseyde, 'Go we, uncle deere';
> And arm in arm inward with hym she wente . . .
> And Pandarus, in ernestful manere,
> Seyde, 'Alle folk, for Godes love, I preye,
> Stynteth [1] right here, and softely yow pleye.' [2]

The lovers are together; the moment of declaration
face to face has come. The full beauty of their sincerity
seems the greater for being set beside the foxing of the
old man, whose practical cynicisms are nevertheless
rooted in a certain warmheartedness.

> 'What that I mene, O swete herte deere?'
> Quod Troilus, 'O goodly fresshe, free, [3]
> That with the stremes of youre eyen cleere
> Ye wolde somtyme frendly on me see. . . .

> 'And I to ben youre verray, humble, trewe,
> Secret, and in my paynes pacient,
> And evere mo desiren fresshly newe
> To serve, and ben ay ylike diligent . . .
> Lo, this mene I, myn owen swete herte.'

And she, not answering him directly, turns to Pandarus,

> Avysyng hire, and hied nought to faste [4]
> With nevere a word, but seyde hym softely,
> 'Myn honour sauf, I wol wel trewely,
> And in swich forme as he gan now devyse,
> Receyven hym fully to my servyse,

---

[1] Stop.
[2] Amuse yourselves.
[3] Free of heart, generous.
[4] But did not hurry too fast.

'Bysechyng hym, for Goddes love, that he
Wolde, in honour of trouthe and gentilesse,
As I wel mene, eke menen wel to me. . . .'

Guillaume de Lorris could not have asked more of them,
or indeed of Pandarus, though here Chaucer's power in
comedy went beyond anything of which Guillaume was
capable.

The part played by Fortune in their tragedy is continually touched throughout the poem, and often casts
a sudden philosophic beauty upon some incident or
remark, with just that power of controlled digression
and sense of universal things that illuminate and deepen
so many of Chaucer's narratives while seeming to delay
them.

Since the poem is concerned with the acts of Fortune,
and these are acts in Time, Chaucer is precise as to the
duration of the loves of his hero and heroine. He is
careful to assure his hearers that their love, secluded
behind the walls of Troy, as in the protected garden of
the *Rose*, continued ever fresh in them, and was the source
of their virtues:

And this encrees of hardynesse and myght
Com hym of love. . . .

But al to litel, welaway the whyle,
Lasteth swich joie, ythonked be Fortune. . . .

For three years they were stayed in their felicity, almost
as if there were no such thing as Time or Chance to touch
them; but for these Criseyde would have been as faithful
and Troilus as fresh as the lovers on the Grecian Urn, yet
able to enjoy and renew the enjoyment of their love.
But three years was to be their date.

Aprochen gan the fatal destynè
That Joves hath in disposicioun . . .

The gold-ytressed Phebus heighe on-lofte
Thriës [1] hadde alle with his bemes clene
The snowes molte, and Zepherus as ofte
Ibrought ayeyn the tendre leves grene,
Syn [2] that the sone of Ecuba the queene
Bigan to love hire first for whom his sorwe
Was al, that she departe sholde a-morwe.

Suddenly in the mid-course of their love, they were to
be separated by circumstances beyond their control.
There was to be an exchange of prisoners; Criseyde was
to be sent from Troy to her father who had gone over
treacherously to the Greeks, in exchange for Antenor, a
Trojan Prince who had been taken in battle. Nothing
could be done to prevent it. For Troilus to seek Hector's
aid or Priam's in the matter and get the exchange
officially quashed would have been to betray his relationship with his mistress, to break secrecy, to sell her honour,
to put the enjoyment of his lady above the service of her
reputation. The same result would have come if he had
fled with her from Troy; it would proclaim their love
and therefore wreck her honour. It was of all things the
forbidden sin in courtly love, and if that love was to
be shown at its best and purest, no such sin could be
allowed to blot it, whatever the consequences. It followed that Fortune and Love had placed Troilus in a
position where he was no longer free to act. The rules
by which he was bound as a lover, and which up till
now had favoured him, had suddenly become chains
upon his power of choice.

Finding himself deprived of freedom to act in a matter

[1] Thrice.   [2] Since.

that touched his whole life, the young lover suddenly perceived his predicament in a new and dreadful light. He was in a universe governed by Necessity. It had been decreed from everlasting that he was to be robbed of Criseyde. He and she had been cast for a Tragedy. It is the moment for his long soliloquy from Boethius, on the impossibility of free will, the core of his tragedy.

Criseyde was led out of Troy, handed over from Troilus into the power of Diomede. From that moment we know little more of her than that she temporized, made promises, evaded them, longed for her first lover, wrote sorrowfully to him, excused herself, and in the end yielded to her second. She had not the courage to make her way back into the beleaguered city. How can we be surprised at this? She only had the qualities appropriate to a secluded garden, for life and love in a protected world. Now she was outside the walls of Troy, outside the garden of the rose. She had been all she ought to have been by the standards of Guillaume de Lorris, but that was not enough in the actual world where there is such a thing as Chance.

Chaucer did not blame her. He would even seek to excuse her, he says, for pity. Nor would he go so far as to say that she gave her love to the thick-shouldered Diomede. That she gave him her body he cannot deny, but more than that he cannot say:

Men seyn—I not—that she yaf [1] hym hire herte.

It was the system itself, not the lovers, that was to blame. Chaucer had been careful to deal justly by the system and it is with compassion and regret that he said farewell to it. He did not condemn it as unchristian.

[1] Gave.

He simply showed that it would not work, even in a
pagan world, and with the noblest protagonists. It was a
way of love that had great beauties and great virtues,
which passed into his hero and heroine; but her virtues
were not enough. It also brought great joys, what might
truly be called bliss, or so Chaucer permits himself to
call it:

> Hire armes smale, hire streghte bak and softe,
> Hire sydes longe, flesshly, smothe, and white
> He gan to stroke, and good thrift bad ful ofte [1]
> Hire snowisshe throte, hire brestes rounde and lite:
> Thus in this hevene he gan hym to delite,
> And therwithal a thousand tyme hire kiste,
> That what to don, for joie unnethe he wiste. . . . [2]

> O blisful nyght, of hem so longe isought,
> How blithe unto hem bothe two thow weere!
> Why nad I swich oon with my soule ybought, [3]
> Ye, or the leeste joië that was theere?
> Awey, thow foule daunger and thow feere,
> And lat hem in this hevene blisse dwelle,
> That is so heigh that al ne kan I telle!

And yet it was brittle. It was not proof against the fatal
accidents of a real world, it could be broken, it could
come to an end.

> Swich fyn [4] hath, lo, this Troilus for love!
> Swich fyn hath al his grete worthynesse!
> Swich fyn hath his estat real above, [5]
> Swich fyn his lust, swich fyn hath his noblesse!
> Swych fyn hath false worldes brotelnesse!

---

[1] Often begged blessings on.
[2] He hardly knew what to do, for joy.
[3] Why had I not bought one such night with my soul?
[4] Such ending.
[5] Such ending had his royal condition above (i.e. after
death).

Having shown it and judged it at its best, in a pagan world, the world of 'Jove, Appollo, of Mars, of swich rascaille', he at last allowed himself to bring into the poem his own world, and the eternal world. If there is no reliance to be placed in love *par amour* there is a real and a serious love in the image of which all lovers were made:

> O yonge, fresshe folkes, he or she,
> In which that love up groweth with youre age,
> Repeyreth hom fro worldly vanytè,[1]
> And of youre herte up casteth the visage[2]
> To thilke God that after his ymage
> Yow made, and thynketh al nys but a faire
> This world,[3] that passeth soone as floures faire.
>
> And loveth hym, the which that right for love
> Upon a crois, oure soules for to beye,
> First starf, and roos,[4] and sit in hevene above;
> For he nyl falsen[5] no wight, dar I seye,
> That wol his herte al holly on hym leye.
> And syn he best to love is, and most meke,
> What nedeth feynede loves for to seke?

This is the ending of the poem, the perfect, the appropriate, the only possible, towards which it had secretly tended from the first stanza, and it comes upon the reader with that sudden surprise by which great writers can convey with force what we should so long have foreseen in reading them, that surprise which gives a character that some call 'inevitability' to a work of art. Quietly Chaucer steps aside from the discarded French philosophy of love and from the Italian tale of

---

[1] Come home (i.e. to God) from worldly vanity.
[2] Cast up the countenance of your heart.
[3] Think the world a fair.
[4] To buy our souls, first died, then rose.
[5] For he will betray no one.

love which he had been so long in telling and gathers his poem into a great doxology, taken from another Italian, Dante, from whom he never took a sentence so easily within his own spiritual reach, or turned one into finer poetry:

> Thow oon, and two, and thre, eterne on lyve,[1]
> That regnest ay in thre, and two, and oon,
> Uncircumscript, and al maist circumscrive,
> Us from visible and invisible foon
> Defende, and to thy mercy, everichon,
> So make us, Jesus, for thi mercy digne,[2]
> For love of mayde and moder thyn benigne.
>   Amen.

Explicit liber Troili et Criseydis.

---

[1] Living eternally.
[2] And, for thy mercy, Jesus, make each one of us worthy of thy mercy.

7

THE RETRACTION

This story has no moral,
This story has no en'.
This story only goes to show
That there ain't no good in men.
He was her man,
He done her wrong.

Frankie and Johnny

IN THESE lines the American popular Muse has summed the loves of Frankie and Johnny, and offered, albeit unconsciously, a perfect description of Chaucer's next poem, *The Legend of Good Women*, or, as he also called it, *The Legend of Cupid's Saints*.

There can be little doubt as to its date and none as to its outward purpose. It is in the form of a collection of tales exemplifying the constancy, sanctity, and martyrdom of women in love, introduced by an allegorical Prologue. As the Prologue is graced with passages in praise of the daisy, imitated from some French poems on the same theme that came into Chaucer's hand in 1386, the poem as a whole cannot be of earlier date, though some of the individual legends may have been written before. The ostensible purpose of the poem is to retract the heresy, implied in the conduct of Criseyde, that women are inconstant and their love untrustworthy. The Prologue allegorically proclaims the poem to be a penance undertaken by the erring poet by order of the Queen, outraged by the slur upon her sex.

All this must be taken into consideration if *The Legend*

of Good Women is to find an intelligible place in the context of Chaucer's maturing genius.

One in whom a genial irony was so subtly developed cannot have failed to taste the piquancy of the situation in which he now found himself. He was to withdraw, at the command of a woman, an opinion about women which a woman had put into his mouth. He was to go back to the baby-language of courtly love. Entering into the spirit of this penance he returned to the allegorical manner. Answer a fool according to her folly.

Male critics were on his side. Thomas Usk did not seem aware that he had uttered any heresy against women and even put praise of the *Troilus* into the mouth of Venus ('his noble sayinges can I not amende') as early as 1387, almost immediately after the 'publication' of the poem. Some thirty years later, Lydgate too wrote thus of it in his *Fall of Princes*:

> Which for to Redë | lovers hem delyte,
> They han ther-Inne | so gret Devocïon.

He too corroborates what the Prologue to *The Legend of Good Women* suggests under the covering of allegory:

> This poete wrot | at Request of the quene,
> A legendë | of parfight hoolynesse
> Off goode women | to Fynden out nyntene
> That did excelle | in bounte and fayrnesse,
> But for his labour | and his besynesse
> Was inportable | his wittes to encoumbre,
> In al this world | to Fynde so greet a noumbre.[1]

The last three lines utter another important truth about the poem. Chaucer never managed to complete the task

---

[1] Except that his labour and trouble insupportably encumbered his wits to find so many.

imposed of spending the remainder of his life, 'yer by
yere',

> In makyng of a glorious legende
> Of goode wymmen, maydenes and wyves,
> That weren trewe in lovyng al hire lyves;
> And telle of false men that hem bytraien. . . .

His wits were 'encumbered', and in the end defeated by
this pious imposition.

A flatter soul than Chaucer's might submissively have
toed the party line and undertaken his recantation
seriously; but,

> Forced to recant our cant, if we have wit,
> Our recantation will have cant in it.

Chaucer, with all appearance of innocence, decided to
toe it to an inward and ironical tune of his own. High
seriousness was laid aside; allegorical fancy-dress was
put on (for the last time) and he entered upon the
exquisite performance of a solemn *badinerie*. Just as a
ballet written and danced in a spirit of graceful comedy
may have moments of serious tenderness and other
moments of burlesque, so *The Legend of Good Women* has
a variety of mood, sentiment, description, comedy, and
light irony to give colour to his monotonous task. The
Prologue is his masterpiece in the allegorical dream-
garden style. His feeling for the freshness of the natural
year, the open air and the green privacy of the little
arbour he had made in his Aldgate garden bring us,
with his reiterated love of books, into closer touch with
his daily life in these last moments of his greatest affluence. Soon after this the house in Aldgate had to be
abandoned, for his fortunes fell.

Although the Prologue is the finest part of the poem,

it is more convenient to begin with the legends themselves in attempting a criticism, for a highly intricate and
scholarly controversy has for many years centred round
the former, and it is as well to keep out of that whirlpool
if possible. If it can be skirted and viewed, but not
entered, the main purpose of this chapter, which is to
place *The Legend of Good Women* in the context of Chaucer's
poetical development, will have been achieved.

Of the nineteen ladies proposed as examples of female
constancy, Chaucer managed to celebrate nine and a
half. Starting with Cleopatra and going on to Thisbe,
Dido, Hypsipyle, Medea, Lucrece, Ariadne, Philomela,
and Phillis, he seems finally to have given up in the
middle of Hypermnestra.

Incipit (says the rubric in three manuscripts) *legenda
Cleopatrie Martyris, Egipti regine*. It is a little startling to
modern taste to find Cleopatra heading the list of faithful
female lovers, the proto-martyr of her sect. The choice
of Medea and Philomela, known for their horrible infan-
ticides, is also odd; but there is evidence for thinking that
in the middle ages they were among the stock examples
of feminine fidelity. Professor Livingston Lowes quotes
L'Epistre au Dieu d'Amours by Christine de Pisan (1399)
and other sources to show that Chaucer's choices were
traditional. This of course would not preclude him from
inward irony. The private joke at the expense of
'authority' was very much to Chaucer's taste, especially
when delivered with solemnity, as when he embarked on
The Ryme of Sir Thopas in *The Canterbury Tales*, traditional,
ludicrous, and gravely given forth.

The poetical tone of these legends, as has been said,
is more varied than their reiterated theme, and considered as a short story, almost any one of them is told

more skilfully and with more flourish of rhetoric and imagery than the classical tales he had embedded in his earlier works. Such a passage as the following battle-piece from the legend of Cleopatra recalls the style and animation of the tourney in *The Knight's Tale*, which, indeed, Chaucer had already written, or drafted, and with a like touch of alliteration to give it vigour.

> With grysely soun out goth the grete gonne,
> And heterly they hurtelen al atones,[1]
> And from the top doun come the grete stones.
> In goth the grapenel, so ful of crokes;
> Among the ropes renne the sherynge-hokes.[2]
> In with the polax preseth he and he;
> Byhynde the mast begynnyth he to fle,
> And out ageyn, and dryveth hym overbord;
> He styngeth hym upon his speres ord. . . .[3]

In the same tale, there is a tenderness in his heroine's last soliloquy which is only less touching than the sorrowing expressions of Criseyde because our feelings have not been so long with Cleopatra. Her tale has been too brief for us to credit or even care for her sincerity. There is not the weight of a long wooing or of an intimately revealed character to engage us at all deeply in what she says; yet they are fine words :

> 'Now, love, to whom my sorweful herte obeyde
> So ferforthly [4] that from that blisful houre
> That I yow swor to ben al frely youre—
> I mene yow, Antonius, my knyght—
> That nevere wakynge, in the day or nyght,
> Ye nere out of myn hertes remembraunce,
> For wel or wo, for carole or for daunce. . . .'

---

[1] Fiercely they hurtled all at once.
[2] Shearing-hooks, to slice through the ropes.
[3] The point of his spear.   [4] Completely.

Shakespeare, basing himself on Chaucer, has turned the tale of Thisbe, second of the Saints of Cupid, into a riot of farce; but the original is pathetic enough:

> How doth this woful Tisbe in this cas!
> How kysseth she his frosty mouth so cold!
> 'Who hath don this, and who hath been so bold
> To sle my leef? [1] O spek, my Piramus!
> I am thy Tisbe, that the calleth thus.'
> And therwithal she lifteth up his hed.
>   This woful man, that was nat fully ded,
> Whan that he herde the name of Tisbe cryen,
> On hire he caste his hevy, dedly yën,
> And doun agayn, and yeldeth up the gost. . . .

What a long way he had come in the practice of narrative poetry can be seen in these examples; he had at least learnt a dexterity in language and speed without breathlessness. It is tempting to say that *Troilus* had taught him how to write with assurance and variety. Yet there is a pervading sense in these stories that Chaucer is indifferent to his heroines and their pretensions in a way he never was to the weakness of Criseyde. He is always in a semi-comic hurry about them, spends little invention on their characters or personalities and presses on to a finish as if he had lost interest or confidence in their importance; for instance:

> I coude folwe, word for word, Virgile,
> But it wolde lasten al to longe while
>   (*Dido*)

> Wel can Ovyde hire letter in vers endyte,
> Which were as now to long for me to wryte.
>   (*Medea*)

---

[1] My darling.

> What shulde I more telle hire compleyning?
> It is so long, it were an hevy thyng.
>   (*Ariadne*)

And so on. There are seventeen such passages in the nine
and a half existing tales; true, these locutions are variations of a trick taken from the *Roman de la Rose*, and
well-known as a rhetorical device, but he had used it
less often in *Troilus*, long as it was.

Another feature that recurs is the deliberate and too-
obvious use of the figures of rhetoric, to heighten the
emotion proper to his tale or moral; consequently a
certain frigidity is sometimes felt. Rhetorical apostrophe
and question cannot move us to pity Lucrece; hardly,
even, to condemn Tarquin:

> Tarquinius, that art a kynges eyr,
> And sholdest, as by lynage and by ryght,
> Don as a lord and as a verray knyght,
> Whi hastow don dispit to chivalrye?
> Whi hastow don this lady vilanye?
> Allas! of the this was a vileyns dede! [1]

At his best he uses rhetoric for comic effect, opening his
attack on the ruffian character of Jason with a piece of
hyperbolical burlesque:

> Thow rote of false lovers, Duc Jasoun,
> Thow sly devourere and confusioun
> Of gentil wemen, tendre creatures . . .
>
> There othere falsen oon, thow falsest two! . . .
>
> Yif that I live, thy name shal be shove
> In English that thy sekte shal be knowe!
> Have at thee, Jason! now thyn horn is blowe!

---

[1] This was a villain's deed of thine (i.e. a lower-class, not a
princely deed).

There are times when a Chaucerian impudence breaks through these tragedies in open laughter:

> She for dispeyr fordide hyreself, allas!
> Swych sorwe hath she, for she besette hire so.
> Be war, ye women, of youre subtyl fo,
> Syn yit this day men may ensaumple se;
> And trusteth, as in love, no man but me.

And that is the moral of the story of Phillis.

In these legends Chaucer never wrote less than well, yet compared to Criseyde it can only be said of his new heroines that 'in the catalogue they go for women'. He had coloured his narratives with rhetoric, urged them forward with cries of haste, enlivened them with humour and touched them with sentiment. Yet he seems to have felt he could do nothing with them; they 'encumbered his wits'. His ninth and last story ends in mid-sentence:

> This tale is seyd for this conclusioun—

but the conclusion, whether in Chaucer's sense of 'moral' or in our own, was never reached; he was about ten stories short of his dictated goal.

In contrast to the cavalier treatment and incomplete performance of the legends is the highly-wrought and personal quality of the Prologue, and it is now necessary to approach that controversial subject, having seen something of the mixture of tenderness and impudence in the legends which it was written to introduce. They are a pointer to our interpretation of the Prologue, which is written in a like mixture of moods, but with far more poetical attention.

The cause of the controversy to which I have alluded

is that the Prologue has come down to us in two versions, one evidently a revision of, and intended to cancel, the other. The question is, which was written first? Which cancels which?

Since the difference between these versions is largely a matter of minor changes in and re-arrangement of passages common to them both, and since there are comparatively few ideas that are present in one version but absent from the other (each version has some lines which the other has not), it is possible to evade the technical argument about priority, until some account of the dream-allegory (which is substantially the same in each) has been given. But for the sake of accurate reference, one slight source of irrelevant confusion may first be cleared up. To distinguish these two versions from each other, Skeat named the one he judged to be the earlier A and the later B. More recent scholars have been convinced that B is earlier than A, and have unfortunately re-named the versions F and G. When they speak of F they are referring to what Skeat calls B. Likewise their G stands for Skeat's A. To make quite certain which version is here under discussion I shall call one AG and the other BF and, for the moment, shelve the question of priority altogether.

Just as *The House of Fame* began with a philosophic inquiry into the nature of dreams, so both Prologues begin, in almost identical phrases, what appears to be a philosophic speculation whether there is pain in Hell and joy in Heaven, but soon resolves itself into an inquiry as to the relative trustworthiness of AUTHORITY and EXPERIENCE. Heaven and Hell are mentioned merely as instances in this, the true argument. It is one of Chaucer's favourite discussions:

A thousand tymes have I herd men telle
That ther ys joy in hevene and peyne in helle,
And I acorde wel that it ys so;
But, natheles, yet wot I wel also
That ther nis noon dwellyng in this contree,
That eyther hath in hevene or helle ybe,
Ne may of hit noon other weyes witen [1]
But as he hath herd seyd, or founde it writen;
For by assay ther may no man it preve.
But God forbede but men shulde leve
Wel more thing then men han seen with yë! [2]
Men shal not wenen every thing a lyë
But yf hymself yt seeth, or elles dooth . . .
           (BF. 1–13. Almost the same in AG)

After this masterpiece of agnostic irony the reflective
poet continues that if the truth of an opinion cannot be
tested by Experience, we can always seek the Authorities,
that is, ancient *books*.

Than mote we [3] to bokes that we fynde,
Thurgh whiche that olde thinges ben in mynde,
And to the doctrine of these olde wyse,
Yeve credence. . . . [4]
Wel ought us thanne honouren and beleve
These bokes, there we han noon other preve.
           (BF. 17–28. Almost the same in AG)

And thus, having skilfully modulated to the second
usual ingredient of his courtly allegories, *books*, he moves
to the expected personal confession:

On bokes for to rede I me delyte,
And to hem yive I feyth and ful credence,
And in myn herte have hem in reverence
So hertely, that ther is game noon
That fro my bokes maketh me to goon,

---

[1] Nor may know of it in any other way.
[2] For no one can prove it by experiment. But God forbid
one should believe no more than one can see.
[3] Then must we.   [4] Give credence.

> But yt be seldom on the holyday,
> Save, certeynly, whan that the month of May
> Is comen, and that I here the foules synge,
> And that the floures gynnen for to sprynge,
> Farewel my bok, and my devocioun!
>
> (BF. 30–9. Almost the same in AG)

and so he is away into his third ingredient, a May morning, and all is set for allegory. The skill and speed of these enharmonic changes from theme to theme freshen their relationship, so that we take the pleasure of watching old steps grow into a new dance. Chaucer goes forth, then, in holiday mood to look at daisies,

> As she that is of alle floures flour,
> Fulfilled of al vertu and honour,
> And evere ilyke, faire and fressh of hewe. . . .
>
> (BF. 53–5. Not in AG)

> My besy gost, that thursteth alwey newe
> To seen this flour so yong, so fressh of hewe,
> Constreyned me . . .
>
> (BF. 103–5. Not in AG)

and after day-long pleasure, he comes home:

> And in a litel herber that I have,
> That benched was on turves fressh ygrave,[1]
> I bad men sholde me my couche make . . .
> I bad hem strawen floures on my bed.
> Whan I was leyd, and had myn eyen hed,[2]
> I fel on slepe within an houre or twoo . . .
>
> (BF. 203–9.   AG. 97–103)

Once asleep, of course, he has a dream; he is back in a meadow (for, as he had explained in *The Parliament of*

---

[1] And in a little arbour that I have with benches of freshly cut turf.

[2] And had closed my eyes.

Fowls, we dream of what we have just been doing), and from afar across the meadow he sees walking

> The god of Love, and in his hand a quene. . . .
> (BF. 213. AG. 145 like in meaning)

Their more than earthly beauty is described, and that of their retinue of nineteen ladies, each of them true in love. To this vision, music is added in a song, formed as a Ballade with an echoing refrain:

> Hyd, Absolon, thy gilte tresses clere;
> Ester, ley thou thy meknesse al adown;
> Hyd, Jonathas, al thy frendly manere;
> Penalopee and Marcia Catoun,
> Make of youre wifhod no comparysoun;
> Hyde ye youre beautës, Ysoude and Eleyne:
> My lady cometh, that all this may disteyne [1] . . .
> (BF. 249–55. Compare AG. 203–9)

This is a masterpiece in an old French style, a style Machault had shown him:

> Ne quier veoir la biaute d'Absalon

and that Villon was later to make famous in his *Ballade des Dames du Temps Jadis,* or, as we know it in Rossetti's perfect translation, *The Ballad of Dead Ladies.* It is the style of the catalogue of lovely names.[2]

In his dream, Chaucer waited, 'as stille as any ston'. He did not have to wait long. The God of Love advances upon him in a divine anger and opens the attack. A worm like Chaucer, he says, has no business near his

[1] Bedim.
[2] The inclusion of Jonathan and Absalom among these ladies I cannot fully explain, but note that Villon includes Alcibiades (Archipiade) among his.

consecrated flower, the daisy, after all those translations
of his that hinder men from serving Love.

> Thou maist yt nat denye,
> For in pleyn text, withouten nede of glose,[1]
> Thou hast translated the Romaunce of the Rose,
> That is an heresye ayeins my lawe,
> And makest wise folk fro me withdrawe . . .
> And of Creseyde thou hast seyd as the lyste,
> That maketh men to wommen lasse triste,[2]
> That ben as trewe as ever was any steel . . .
>   (BF. 327–34. Much the same in AG. 253–66)

This judgement of the God must give us pause; *The
Romance of the Rose* was no heresy. On the contrary it was
the very gospel of Love, unless Cupid was referring to
the additions by club-foot Jean de Meun; but, so far
as we know, Chaucer had not made a translation
of that part. However, as we shall presently see, the
God of Love did not know so much about books as he
pretended.

In this passage Chaucer has artfully circled back to
the topic of *books*, with which he had opened his poem.
It was a return to his boomerang technique for throw-
ing forth an allegory, such as we have already seen in
his earlier work. The question concerning Heaven and
Hell (a mere illustration) is never mentioned again, but
the question of Authority is now, immediately, brought
forward by the God of Love, thus linking the main body
of the poem with its philosophical introduction, in
Chaucer's usual manner. Having abused Chaucer for
translating the wrong, heretical books (*Troilus* and the

---

[1] For clearly and without need of a commentary.
[2] And you have said as you pleased of Criseyde, which
makes men trust women less.

Roman de la Rose), he now recommends by name the books Chaucer ought to have translated:

> Was there no good matere in thy mynde,
> Ne in alle thy bokes ne coudest thow nat fynde
> Som story of wemen that were goode and trewe?
> Yis, God wot, sixty bokes olde and newe
> Hast thow thyself, alle ful of storyes grete
> That bothe Romayns and ek Grekes trete
> Of sundry wemen, which lyf that they ladde,
> And evere an hundred goode ageyn oon badde.
> This knoweth God, and alle clerkes eke. . . .
>
> What seyth Valerye, Titus, or Claudyan?
> What seith Jerome agayns Jovynyan?
> How clene maydenes, and how trewe wyves,
> How stedefaste widewes durynge alle here lyves,
> Telleth Jerome, and that nat of a fewe,
> But, I dar seyn, an hundred on a rewe . . .
>
> > (AG. 270–85. Not in BF)

Let us pause to answer the God's questions. What, in fact, had 'Valerye, Titus and Claudyan' said? What had St. Jerome said against Jovinian?

Titus is Titus Livy, the historian of chaste Lucrece. Claudian is the Roman author of a poem on the Rape of Proserpine. These would do well enough to correct the supposed heresies of Chaucer. But what about Valerius and St. Jerome? There are two candidates for Valerius, one a very feeble one, the other a hot favourite. He might be Valerius Maximus who wrote in praise of Portia. But his claims must, I think, give way to those of Walter Map who wrote the *Epistola Valerii ad Rufinum ne uxorem ducat*. This work was much in Chaucer's mind and closely associated there with the fourth of these recommended authors, St. Jerome. The Saint's work here referred to is thus described by Tyrwhitt: 'The holy Father, by way of recommending celibacy, has exerted all his learning and eloquence (and certainly he was not deficient in either) to collect together and aggravate whatever he could find to the prejudice of the female sex.' It thus chimes in and makes a pair with Walter Map's cynical advice to Rufinus on the same subject. The association of these two anti-feminist works in Chaucer's mind is certain from his free use of them both, side by side, in the Preamble to *The Wife of Bath's Tale*. Just as her problem of weighing Experience against Authority had also started the *Legend*, so now two of the principal books on which her handling of matrimony is based, are at the heart of this Prologue to a legend of faithful wives. Here is a quotation from St. Jerome to illustrate his point of view: '*Non hic de meretrice, non de adultera dicitur, sed amor mulieris generaliter accusatur, qui semper insatiabilis est ... Per tria movetur terra, quartum autem non potest ferre: si servus regnet, et stultus si saturetur panibus, et odiosa uxor si habeat bonum virum.*' [1]

The attitude of Walter Map may be discerned in the anecdote Valerius tells Rufinus of a man who wept because three of his wives had hanged themselves on a tree in his garden. His friend begged a cutting.

Such were the books recommended by the God of Love! These were the 'Authorities' on the fidelity of

---

[1] I am not here speaking of the harlot, nor of the adulteress, but inveighing against the love of woman in general, which is always insatiable. ... The world is staggered by three monstrosities, a fourth however would be intolerable: when a servant is in command, when a fool is clogged with food, and when an odious wife has a good husband.

women that were to be trusted when experience failed, when one

> Ne may of hit noon other weyes witen,
> But as he hath herd seyd, or founde it writen.
>   (BF and AG. 6–7)

The meek-eyed poet of Love accepted all this advice in apparent good faith. It was not for him to bandy words with his sovereign, as the dream-Queen was quick to point out when he attempted to put up a defence for the translation of the *Rose* and *Troilus*:

> 'Lat be thyn arguynge,
> For Love ne wol nat countrepleted be
> In ryght ne wrong; [1] and lerne that at me!'
>   (BF. 475–7. AG. 465–7)

And then she imposes her penance; we know it already:

> 'Now wol I seyn what penance thou shalt do
> For thy trespas, and understonde yt here:
> Thow shalt, while that thou lyvest, yer by yere,
> The moste partye of thy tyme spende
> In makyng of a glorious legende
> Of goode wymmen, maydenes and wyves,
> That weren trewe in lovyng al hire lyves;
> And telle of false men that hem bytraien . . .'.
>   (BF. 479–86. AG. 469–76)

And, in one version, she adds what amounts to a command that he must add a personal compliment and dedication to Queen Anne of Bohemia, whose opinions (if we may trust Lydgate) she voices:

> 'And whan this book ys maad, yive it the quene,
> On my byhalf, at Eltham or at Sheene.' [2]
>   (BF. 496–7. Not in AG)

---

[1] Will not be argued with, right or wrong.
[2] There were royal palaces at Eltham and Sheen.

This Queen Alcestis of the vision in the Prologues is a more reliable authority on books than King Cupid. She seems to know everything that Chaucer had written up to date, and gives a very useful little bibliography of a conversational kind:

> He made the book that hight the Hous of Fame,
> And eke the Deeth of Blaunche the Duchesse,
> And the Parlement of Foules, as I gesse,
> And al the love of Palamon and Arcite
> Of Thebes, thogh the storye ys knowen lyte;
> And many an ympne [1] for your halydayes,
> That highten balades, roundels, virelayes;
> And, for to speke of other holynesse,
> He hath in prose translated Boece,
> And maad the lyf also of Seynt Cecile . . .
>   (BF. 417–26. AG. (with one addition) 405–16)

But then she had been very kind to him throughout and had even sought to excuse him before the angry God on the ground that Chaucer did not know what he was talking about:

> And taketh non hed of what matere he take, [2]
> Therfore he wrot the Rose and ek Criseyde
> Of innocence, and nyste what he seyde.
>   (BF first line only, 365. AG. 343–5)

Once again Chaucer the Simpleton is a main character in his allegory, but this time an ironical simpleton.

The Prologues end with the revelation, given by Cupid, that this kindly Queen is Alcestis herself, whose flower, the daisy, Chaucer had spent the day adoring. Her last command is given as the poet wakes and turns once more to the making of a book, as at the end of *The Parliament of Fowls*:

---

[1] Hymn for your (i.e. Cupid's) holy days.
[2] Takes no notice of the subject he has chosen.

'At Cleopatre I wol that thow begynne
And so forth, and my love so shalt thow wynne. . . .'
And with that word, of slep I gan awake,
And ryght thus on my Legende gan I make.
(AG. 542–5. Expanded in BF. 566–79)

Either of these versions of the Prologue is a little masterpiece, and has that milky, morning freshness that belongs
to no poet so much as to Chaucer. Both tell the same
story (with a few trifling variations of detail), at approxi-
mately the same length, and both are shot through with
so great a variety of moods that to name and instance
them all would be impossible. From the ironical buffoonery of making the God of Love unwittingly recom-
mend St. Jerome as a champion of faithful ladies, to
passages of description that recall the *Primavera* of Botticelli, or the intimate glimpses he vouchsafes of private
life in London, there is all the changeable beauty of an
opal.

The subtlest ingenuity in the poem, however, remains
the way in which he has contrived his retraction. He
heralds his return to orthodoxy by opening verses of the
blandest agnosticism, and in one version at least attempts
the same joke on his Court-audience as Chanticleer was
to bring off successfully against Pertelote. The passage
about the books of St. Jerome and Walter Map, so
artfully led up to and disguised by the innocent Livy and
Claudian, is a piece of impudence towards Queen Anne
on the same pattern as Chanticleer's remark to Pertelote:

For al so siker as *In principio*,
Mulier est hominis confusio,—
Madame, the sentence of this Latyn is,
'Womman is mannes joye and al his blis.'

It may be that the Queen was less gullible than Pertelote.

Or it may be that some tattling tongue about the Court apprised her of Chaucer's subtle piece of impudence,

> For in youre court is many a losengeour,[1]
> And many a queynte totelere [2] accusour. . . .
> (AG. 328–9. BF. 352–3)

and the offending passage about books was removed in revision. Or it may be that the passage was an after-thought of impudence and added in revision; all depends on which version was the earlier.

The debate as to priority has been long and intricate and is as yet unsettled. The most recent voices have been given in favour of BF. But the controversy need not be entered here for it cannot be decisive in our estimate of Chaucer's poetical talent. It is true that some scholars favouring the priority of BF have thought the poem wholly serious, a genuine heartfelt proclamation of Chaucer's faith in the truth of women ('tender creatures'), and have marshalled their arguments and interpreta-tions accordingly. But this can only be maintained in the teeth of St. Jerome and Walter Map. Whether or not the Queen knew what these two had written of her sex, Chaucer certainly knew and delighted in it. To suppose *The Legend of Good Women*, with its agnostic introduction, is to be taken *au pied de la lettre*, as if it belonged to the early days of *The Book of the Duchess*, is like not knowing whether there is any salt in the soup.

The very great beauty of his vision of the Aldgate garden, its private arbour and fresh new turf and sense of homely quiet is invaded by another, more Botticellian, beauty when the God of Love and his attendant Ladies come in their flower-crowns. Privacy yields to the divine

---

[1] Flatterer.   [2] Tale-bearing.

presences, not the less splendid for the overtones of comedy in their conversation, much as it was to yield, in the garden of old January, when Pluto and his Queen Proserpina come there to walk, as is told in *The Merchant's Tale*. In each the blend of irony and romantic feeling make a kind of harmony for which no poet has so delicate a touch as Chaucer.

The Prologues to *The Legend of Good Women* are the top of his allegorical writing, as they are his farewell word to allegory. They are also his first attempt in a new shape of poem, the shape that was to grow into *The Canterbury Tales*. It sets a scene out of which a succession of tales can pour. Once or twice before he had tried a short-story, such as was the story of Ceix and Halcyon in *The Book of the Duchess*; but short-story-telling had not yet matured into his pre-eminent gift in poetic form. Now this gift was declaring itself, and if it seems still a little cramped in these legends of good women, it may be because he was working out an air with variations, an air not of his own choice, perhaps not to his taste, and one that set a formal limit to his even richer gift of remarking truthfully on human nature.

8

BIOGRAPHICAL (III)
(1386–1400)

FORTUNE'S WHEEL had turned with sudden fury for the poet in December 1386. From his 'realm of great nobleye' in the Customs Office and the Petty Customs, whose duties he had the impressive power to delegate, 'Fortune awey hym carf', and the next we hear about him is that he felt himself in danger of being sued for debt. It cannot have been a happy time for him; in October the house in Aldgate had been given up, with its little arbour and the fresh turf he had planted there; perhaps he was no longer in a position to bid 'men sholde me my couche make' and order servants to strew flowers on his bed, and it is thought that at this time, or shortly after in the following year, Philippa his wife died. His patron, and hers, John of Gaunt, was out of the country on one of his mad military adventures; on 7 July 1386 he had sailed from Plymouth to Portugal, in the hope of becoming King of Castille. He was away for three years, and though he failed of his long dream to be crowned, he made a good thing of it financially, for the Castillians bought him off at a heavy price. All this was of little help to Chaucer, for in the Duke's absence his brother the Duke of Gloucester, with whom Chaucer seems to have had no connexion, took control of the government at home with full support from the murmuring Commons. Richard II was only twenty, much

in the hands of his unpopular minions. Very ugly
rumours were abroad. His uncle Gloucester called up
the memory of what had happened to Edward II for
like offences, and even had the records of his deposition
read out in Parliament, so that precedent could, if
necessary, be observed. Apart from political commotions,
London was at this time disturbed by the hourly expectation of a naval invasion by Charles VI of France, who
had collected an armada at Sluys.

One would think it an uncomfortable year for citizens,
especially for a middle-aged poet who had lost his income and position and was being pressed by creditors.
Chaucer remained cheerful. He was being visited by
thoughts far more important for England and himself
than depositions and armadas. The trouble with Gloucester led Richard ultimately to have him murdered, the
first positive step towards his own violent end and the
Lancastrian usurpation. But at long last even the Wars
of the Roses blew over, and their memory, from the
dreadful thing it was to the Tudors, has become almost
picturesque material for the second (in time) of our
greatest poets. The Wars of the Roses have faded, but
we still have *The Canterbury Tales*, and the *Histories* of
Shakespeare.

The Canterbury Tales were now beginning to fill
Chaucer's mind. His long and business-like observation
of life round the Port of London was suddenly turning
into a new kind of poetry, as new to the world as it was
to him.

Early in 1389 there came a rumour from abroad that
the great Duke was returning. At a meeting of the Privy
Council held in May, King Richard, who had wind of
this, mildly asked his uncle Gloucester how old he now

was. Gloucester, suspecting nothing more than another
of his nephew's irritating tricks, replied that he believed
his Majesty was twenty-three. Then, said the King, he
was now old enough to manage his own affairs, and
promptly called upon his overbearing governors to
resign their offices of State. Had he not at once filled
them most judiciously, instead of (as was expected)
cramming in his favourites again, this *coup d'état* might
not have come off; as it was, the stroke was for the time
successful.

It looks as if Richard liked Chaucer and valued his
poetry. Nothing is more probable, for like other of our
less popular kings, Richard was a man of taste and
temperament. Shakespeare's picture of him is most
faithful, more so perhaps than any other of his portraits
of English kings. He was poetical and, as he was
implacably vindictive against his enemies, so he was
strong for his friends. In July 1389 Chaucer was appointed Clerk of the Works at Westminster Palace, the
Tower of London and elsewhere during his good
behaviour, with power to impress labour, to purvey
materials and carriage, to pursue absconding workmen,
to arrest contrary people, to make inquisition as to
materials embezzled, and to sell the branches and bark
of trees felled for timber; all this at a salary of two
shillings a day, or in our money roughly £1,400 a year.
In November John of Gaunt returned. Chaucer's nadir
was past; Fortune's wheel was rising steadily once more.
For the rest of his life he was to enjoy royal favour and a
modest private affluence.

As an overseer of public works he seems to have been
as capable as he had shown himself in the Customs. If
as a poet he ignored the affairs of his day, as a servant of

the Crown he did his duty. In 1390 he was commissioned to survey the walls, ditches, sewers, and bridges on the bank of the Thames between Greenwich and Woolwich. This was in March; in May he was put in charge of the erection of scaffolds for the King and Queen to watch the jousting in Smithfield. In July he was employed on a three-year contract to repair St. George's Chapel at Windsor; in 1391 he was appointed Sub-Forester of the Forest of North Petherton in Somerset. In 1393 he received £10 for good service to the King during that year: in 1394, a pension of £20 for life; in 1395, a scarlet robe, trimmed with fur, from Bolingbroke, son of John of Gaunt, and later Henry IV. It was the poet's second story of success. The only recorded misadventure of this period in his life was a brief bout of highway robbery of which he was the victim. He appears to have been set upon and robbed two or three times within three or four days. It was in September 1390; 'at the foul oak at Hatcham'. He was robbed of a £10 horse, goods to the value of a hundred shillings and £20. 6s. 8d. in cash. The loss of so much public money (for he lost none of his own) was officially excused in the following year.

Jottings of this kind, which are all that remain for these years, do not make up a life, still less the life of a poet; but they are enough to show him still active in minor capacities in the public world; in his private world he was writing *The Canterbury Tales*. That was certainly his main employment. He also wrote a few lighter pieces, of which the best is *L'Envoy to Bukton*, if we except the incomparable *Merciless Beauty*, the most graceful bombshell he ever addressed to a lady in the courts of love. It explodes in the last stanza:

> Sin I fro Love escaped am so fat,
> I never thenk to ben his prison lene; [1]
> Sin I am free, I counte him not a bene. . . .

He was getting old. Not too old for love by courtly
standards (which allowed it in a man up to sixty), but
too old on his own account to be a poet. Both the
Complaint to Venus and *L'Envoy to Scogan* complain of
his age and how it has dulled his poetry. The former is a
free translation of a poem by Otes de Granson, whom
it mentions; but the passage about his age is Chaucer's:

> For elde, that in my spirit dulleth me,
> Hath of endyting al the subtiltè
> Wel nygh bereft out of my remembraunce;
> And eke to me it ys a gret penaunce,
> Syth rym in Englissh hath such skarsetè. . . .
>
> (*Complaint of Venus*)

In his earlier years he had found no such difficulty; the
rhymes fell pat enough then, as he tells Scogan:

> But wel I wot, thow wolt answere and saye:
> 'Lo, olde Grisel lyst to ryme and playe!'
>
> Nay, Scogan, say not so, for I m'excuse—
> God helpe me so!—in no rym, dowteles,
> Ne thynke I never of slep to wake my muse,
> That rusteth in my shethe stille in pees.
> While I was yong, I put hir forth in prees; [2]
> But al shal passe that men prose or ryme;
> Take every man hys turn, as for his tyme.
>
> (*L'Envoy to Scogan*)

---

[1] This line in Skeat's edition as well as in Robinson's reads:

> I never thenk to ben in his prison lene;

but for my emendation I am indebted to Professor J. R. R.
Tolkien, who points out that it improves both scansion and
meaning—viz. 'I never think to be his thin prisoner' instead
of 'I never think to be in his prison thin'

[2] I gave her plenty of exercise.

If in this poem he was meaning literal truth, he must by that time have abandoned his last masterpiece, *The Canterbury Tales*, unfinished and unfinishable. He had 'taken his turn'.

L'Envoy to Bukton has a flash of the old irony; it is a piece of advice to those about to get married.

> And therefore, though I highte [1] to expresse
> The sorwe and wo that is in mariage,
> I dar not writen of it no wikkednesse,
> Lest I myself falle eft in swich dotage. [2] . . .

Philippa was ten years dead; but perhaps he was not thinking of her so much as of the Wife of Bath:

> I wol nat seyn how that yt is the cheyne
> Of Sathanas, on which he gnaweth evere. . . .

> The Wyf of Bathe I pray yow that ye rede
> Of this matere that we have on honde.
> God graunte yow your lyf frely to lede
> In fredam; for ful hard is to be bonde.

It was at about this time (1397) that the daily pitcher of wine from the King became an annual tun; his endings, like his beginnings, have the association of wine, as if Fortune were making her own circling pattern of his story and gathering up the threads at the finish. Somehow he continued unable to live within his income and as late as 1398 was once more in danger of being sued for debt. However, in the next year he received an additional pension of twenty marks, and took the lease of a tenement in the garden of St. Mary's Chapel in Westminster Abbey. A new King had come to the throne through bloodshed; but he was the son of John

---

[1] Promised to express.
[2] Fall once more into such dotage.

of Gaunt and the family favour held with the old poet and servant. Chaucer addressed a poem to him, complaining of the lightness of his purse. It was probably the last thing he ever wrote, and like his first long poem a tribute to the Lancasters that had so faithfully looked after him. As ever, in spite of the violence of the times, his poem is politically somewhat colourless. He contents himself with a conventional acceptance of the claims on succession to the Crown that had been heard in Parliament after the deposition of Richard. If he felt any qualms about their legality, he did not express them. He was no fanatic, he accepted things as they were:

> O conqueror of Brutes Albyon,[1]
> Which that by lyne and free eleccion [2]
> Been verray kyng, this song to yow I sende;
> And ye, that mowen alle oure harmes amende,
> Have mynde upon my supplicacion!
>
> *(Complaint to his Purse)*

If in this he seems less noble than gratitude to his former patron Richard might have demanded, it may be suggested that in common with most of his fellow-countrymen he could not feel heroic on behalf of so wayward a ruler, for all his patronage of the arts. Also he was getting old.

In the next year he drew a part of his pension in February, and again in June, and those are the last entries in the record; he did not live the year out. His tomb, in St. Benet's Chapel, Westminster Abbey, bears the date of his death, 25 October 1400.

---

[1] The England of King Brutus, supposed Trojan founder of Britain.

[2] By hereditary succession and free election, the gist of the formula used on behalf of Henry IV's seizure of the throne.

9

THE PROLOGUE TO THE CANTERBURY TALES

This happy breed of men, this little world. . . .
Richard II

EVERY POEM of Chaucer's that we have considered derived from some work or works in other tongues, though each had touches of a kind of novelty that we have learnt to call 'Chaucerian'. As his work matured these touches became more frequent and pervasive. His way of looking at things changed the things he looked at more and more, and every change seemed to lift them and the poem, for a moment at least, into what still seems a present actuality and away from literary convention. We have come, in the course of time, to value the flavour of actuality above almost all flavours in our reading, and this is one reason why Chaucer seems so 'modern'.

Yet if none of these poems could be called wholly 'modern' in that some of their poetical pleasures depend upon our power to recognize and enjoy a host of medieval ways of thought, *The Prologue* to *The Canterbury Tales* needs no spiritual glossary. It at once fills the imagination with the simple clarities of daily fact. Chaucer's astounding originality had at last taken the lead in its long and loving partnership with tradition, his trust in what he saw and heard in the world about him had lovingly invaded and conquered the domain of poetry. Experience had wedded Authority, and perhaps achieved sovereignty in the marriage.

The result was a new sort of poetical truth, the creation of a poetry of fact by a wise, sure-eyed, and sensitive selection of daily detail, mellowed and harmonized by a humane and often an amused approval, qualified wherever approval was withdrawn by an ironical wit. It was a new way of looking at people.

This kind of vision that we have seen so gradually maturing came to sudden fullness towards the year 1386 and brought with it a number of enormous ideas that, once embodied, seem the simplest possible; but how or why or in what order they came to him we do not know.

Nothing forbids us to believe that the Canterbury Pilgrimage idea sprang upon him in an instant with all its inner logic intuitively complete. Or it may have dawned gradually. He has not told us. My guess would be that it came to him, or began to come, as he was tidying up his papers for the move from his house in Aldgate. He had time on his hands, dismissed as he had been from his comptrollerships, time to wonder what could be made of a miscellaneous heap of manuscripts such as his tale of Palamon and Arcite, his Life of St. Cecilia, his little clutch of 'tragedies', his story of Griselda. They must in some moods have seemed a job lot. Was there no way in which their differing qualities could be bound into the unifying strength of a single work? And could anything be done with 'Melibee'?

There were many collections of stories in existence, some of which cannot but have been known to Chaucer. Boccaccio had written no less than three, the *Ameto*, the *Filocolo* and the *Decameron*. John Gower, co-dedicatee of *Troilus and Criseyde*, was even then at work on the *Confessio Amantis*, a collection strung together, not to say ham-strung, by their single preposterous theme of

Courtly Passion jacketed in the Seven Deadly Sins, each tale an example of some sin or sub-sin, as if Cupid had borrowed Christianity to sermonize his incompatible cult. Chaucer himself had attempted, in *The Legend of Good Women*, to rope a set of tales together on the very cord that ultimately strangled them, the constancy of women.

Yet it could not be denied that a collection of stories gained something from a unifying principle, something dear to Chaucer with his concern for poetical form. But it was gained at the risk of monotony and restriction. It leaned towards the ridiculous and the literary and seemed to exclude actuality altogether.

Chaucer now found a solution to this problem so obvious that everyone else had missed it. It was to unite the diversity of his tales by allotting them to a diversity of tellers joined in some likely common purpose. This, analytically speaking, is the root-principle of *The Canterbury Tales*.

He found his diversity of creatures in the circumstantial world about him, God's world, his own world, the world of the Port of London, the world of England itself. There lay the right raw material for all his special gifts. And so a second organizing principle or idea becomes discernible in the huge conception, namely to paint a National Portrait Gallery.[1]

He did not underline this idea. It is simply there, for every reader to infer. In all our literature there is not such another picture of a whole society, and Chaucer

---

[1] But this of course did not prevent him from touching up some of his portraits with bits out of his favourite books. The table-manners of the Prioress, for instance, are taken from the *Roman de la Rose*.

contrived it in some two-and-thirty characters and 860 lines.

It was second nature with him that his sense of actuality should mingle with his sense of hierarchy. He presented his characters in the jumble and haphazardry of life, with a mild apology for his neglect of rank. All was to seem fortuitous, and yet all the ranks and vocations, the trades and the professions were there. What Shakespeare would have called 'degree' was omnipresent, though in a deliberately disordered chain, and the historian can rebuild out of *The Prologue* the twin ladders of Church and State as they then were, with scarcely a rung missing.

A high kind of gentle blood is seen in the Knight and his son, a lesser somewhat emulous gentry in the land-owning Franklin. The learned professions appear in the Serjeant-at-Law and the Doctor. The Merchant stands for the upper reaches of commerce, for the new class of wool-exporters and exchange-manipulators, beginners in capitalism, while the Haberdasher and his associates represent the slightly smaller fry of London traders, though each

Was shaply for to been an alderman.

The Wife of Bath, a provincial and a woman, was a cloth-maker, an expert in the newest and most important of England's industries at the time. Another provincial, this time a sea-dog, was the Shipman, owner and master-mariner. All these were of some rank. They would have servants at home, they would exact and enjoy a high local prestige. Next below them were the churl-folk, of whom the Miller was the grandest, his own master, with the coveted right to work a mill, a man to give himself airs. The swaggering Simkin of *The Reve's Tale* was such another, with a wife

> as digne as water in a dich.

Then came the servant class: upper servants like the Manciple and the Reve, lower servants like the Yeoman and the Cook, each pair representing Town and Country between them. At the absolute bottom of the social scale came the country Ploughman, and bottom though he was, he was nearest among these lay-folk to the Knight in generous Christianity. They were both *animae naturaliter christianae*.

The Church was hardly less exactly represented. The Monk from his monastery, the Prioress from her convent, her attendant Priests, the village Parson, and the roaming Friar, sufficiently covered the more usual religious categories. The courtly pretensions of the Prioress and the humble origins of the Parson (he was the Ploughman's brother) showed the comparative unimportance of personal rank in the religious life. Somewhere between laity and ecclesiastics came the Clerk of Oxford to represent the Universities, a poor scholar who as yet had got no benefice. At an infinite moral and social depth below all these came the Pardoner and the Summoner. It is true that the Pardoner might enjoy a certain prestige founded on superstition, but his natural level was with the Summoner, 'his freend and his compeer'. Both were laymen, hangers-on of the Church, and hated.

For all the methodical selection and artistic ingenuity that must have gone to the presenting of these characters, it was an almost greater triumph to have made them seem so gloriously haphazard in their congregation. This

I

was partly contrived by the stroke of genius that could imagine the only two places in England where they would all be likely to meet on equal terms, an Inn and a Cathedral, and the circumstance, a pilgrimage, that could credibly unite them in a common purpose. The journey between the two would be the occasion for their diverse tales. Chaucer himself could be on such a pilgrimage; once again he could place himself inconspicuously at the heart of his poem. He had found a form absolutely perfect for his special talents.

But there is something deeper than either form or talent in *The Prologue* to *The Canterbury Tales*. That deeper thing was his attitude to the created world. The devices of craftsmanship and ingenuity, and the happy thoughts that embellish a large design are only the servants or children of such vision. It took a Chaucer not only to hit upon them, but to handle them, and that handling-power seems to me centred in the Chaucer who had written in *The House of Fame*, so many years before,

> 'O God!' quod y, 'that made Adam,
> Moche ys thy myght and thy noblesse!'

He had always taken joy in the created world, a joy tinged with quizzical wonder. The simplicity of his delight in things for being what they were was qualified by an acute and questioning intelligence, and this in turn qualified by a gravely comic personal humility. So bland, so unselfconscious, so mild a spectator of God's plenty could be simple without *naïveté*, romantic without foolishness, ironical without cruelty. He seems omnivorous and yet a dainty feeder. The freshness of his gaze is like that of a man who can see what is familiar to him without losing the vividness of a child's vision. Nothing is blurred, every colour is as true as in heraldry or in a primitive painting. His eye, 'gilding the object whereupon it gazeth', at the same time perceives with a perfectly mature intelligence, deeply pleased, amused, and upon occasion touched. The perfect good manners of his observation, and of his observations, has a Christian courtliness derived from the poetry of dream and a robustness derived from his gradual awakening into a sunlit actuality. It was the April of the world, to him no cruel month. Such a vision, crisped by wit, now centred itself on men and women. He proceeded to invent a way of describing them.

He had already invented one way in *Troilus and Criseyde*, where the characters grow into action from within. Pandarus creates himself out of conversation and that inner wiliness of his. But this way of presenting character is a slow one, suited only to a few protagonists engaged at deep levels of feeling. It would not suit a group of pilgrims casually met. Chaucer now hit upon another way of presentation, the selection and adding up of outward detail into the prime number that makes a human being, as he appears objectively, with no more inner life (and no less) than men and women seem to have when we meet and talk to them fortuitously and are struck by their personalities.

As in our own lives, at some gathering, we are variously struck by one or another, so Chaucer. He varied his presentation from the full-length portrait to the thumb-nail sketch. Of some, their appearance, personal history, likes, dislikes, qualities, and aptitudes are described in detail, sometimes with a snatch of conversation, such as we have learnt to expect from him. 'And I seyde his

opinion was good', was his comment on the opinions of
the Monk. Apparently grave, it rings across the centuries
in Chaucer's accent of sardonic innocence.

As the casual is an ingredient of the actual, he has a
trick in some descriptions of pointing observation by a
series of footnotes or afterthoughts; thus ends the
description of the Monk, for instance:

> He was nat pale as a forpyned goost.[1]
> A fat swan loved he best of any roost.
> His palfrey was as broun as is a berye.

Only one character is presented by the technique of
Troilus and Criseyde, and that one of the most important,
Harry Bailey the Host. Like Pandarus he is built up
out of what he does and says rather than what he looks
like. The same miracle of clarity and fullness is achieved.

There is some reason for thinking Harry Bailey and
one or two others were portraits taken from actual men,
well-known in London at the time. The Subsidy Rolls
of Southwark record what might be called the 'black
market' practices of one 'Henri Bayliff, ostyler' in 1375-6,
and he may well have sat unconsciously for Chaucer's
portrait. Thomas Pynchbeck, Serjeant-at-Law in 1376
and Baron of the Exchequer in 1388, may be the original
of Chaucer's Man of Law:

> Ther koude no wight *pynche* at his writyng.[2]

If so, this is Chaucer's only plain pun.[3] Proust tells us
that a book is a great cemetery in which, for the most

[1] Tormented soul.

[2] No one could find fault with what he wrote. (Italics are
mine.)

[3] Except perhaps

> So whan this Calkas knew by calkulynge.
> > (*Troilus and Criseyde,* I, 71.)

part, the names on the tombstones have been effaced. It is a paradox that Henri Bayliff and Thomas Pynchbeck are ghosts, and their portraits, if portraits they were, flesh and blood. But it is possible to hunt too far in factual record to trace what are essentially imaginations. To search the registers of Bath for a woman named Alison five times married is to look for the bones of Pharaoh's lean kine.

The spiritual power of a zest for actual life shows itself not only in the plenty and variety of his pilgrims, but especially in their normality. He did not exaggerate or look for freaks, he delighted in the world as he found it. Incapable of stale vision, he also had the perennial happiness of touch described by Dryden as belonging only to a master, 'to draw a full face, and to make the nose and cheeks stand out, and yet not employ any depth of shading. This is the mystery of that noble trade, which yet no master can teach his apprentice.' Zest in experience and clarity in language are the unflagging qualities of *The Prologue*. 'Execution', said Blake, 'is the chariot of Genius.'

Chaucer's delight in normality is what chiefly differentiates him from Dickens, with whom he has so often been compared. Dickens is a master of the eccentric. When we think of him a wonderful host of fabulously erratic figures comes to mind, adorable grotesques, monsters of iniquity, paragons of pathos, of optimism, cunning, meanness, benevolence. Everything is in untameable, romantic excess. Micawbers, Mantalinis, Fagins, Pickwicks, Pecksniffs, and a hundred other giants of comic or terrible eccentricity are spawned by his unflagging imagination. The very waiters at wayside inns, the tramps on the road, have their violent idiosyncrasies. But Chaucer's world is almost freak-free, his characters perfectly life-size. Only the Wife of Bath seems larger and louder than life. But she is a special case.

The frame of the poem into which ambled Chaucer's characters from the normal world was circular. Ever since the *Book of the Duchess* Chaucer had favoured a poetry that circled back to its starting-point, one that ended in its beginnings. Now, in late life, he planned another boomerang poem, with a trajectory from London to Canterbury and back. This, he supposed, would allow him room for 120 tales. It is a measure of the confidence he felt in his great idea and in his power to complete it. Thirty pilgrims, including himself, two stories from each on the way out, two on the way back, and a dinner for the best. It was a wide elbow-room.

Chaucer never completed his circle. He left nine great arcs of it, gapped and imperfectly joined. If the caval-cade reached Canterbury in the pilgrim mood prepared by *The Parson's Tale*, nine of his tellers had been crowded out altogether with no chance of a victorious dinner, and only Chaucer himself had been allowed two tales, one interrupted.

Others had been interrupted too; *The Monk's Tale* had been brought to a timely, the Cook's and the Squire's to an untimely end. All these interruptions, save that of the Cook, were a part of Chaucer's artistry in the actual. Simpleton-Chaucer could be rudely told to stop by Harry Bailey:

'Thy drasty rymyng is nat worth a toord!'

But the Monk, having asserted his dignity by a show of serious learning, needed no less a person than the Knight

to check his tediousness. The Squire, gathering himself
for an almost endless recital,

> First wol I telle yow of Cambyuskan . . .
> And after wol I speke of Algarsif, . . .
> And after wol I speke of Cambalo . . .
> And ther I lefte I wol ayeyn bigynne. . . .

is choked by the praises of the Franklin, the only person present, except his proud Father, fit to interrupt
him. Human endurance and the decencies of hierarchy
were in this way both respected. The truncation of
The Cook's Tale, however, remains unexplained, and I
for one regret it more than the interruption of the Squire,
deplored by Milton. The greatest interruption of all,
however, was not to a tale but to the cavalcade itself.
Actuality sweeps in at a gallop with the Canon and his
Yeoman. It is almost the finest comic surprise in the
poem, a rushing in of the outer world into the world of
imagination, life breaking in upon plan haphazardly
with the bit between its teeth.

But the poem was never completed. Had it been so,
perhaps every tale would have suited its teller. As things
are there are a few anomalies. Yet for the most part they
fit so well that one might say the tales grow out of the
characters and the characters grow out of the tales. And
both grow out of the Prologue and the linking colloquies
between tales.

Within this living framework of an English actuality
are placed the no less living fantasies of Europe; for
if *The Prologue* is a cross-section of fourteenth-century
English life, the *Tales* are a cross-section of fourteenth-
century imagination through Christendom.

Romance-Epic in the High Style as in *The Knight's*

Tale, and in the Low, as in *Sir Thopas*, scurrilous *fabliaux*, saints' lives, tragic anecdotes, Aesopian fable, Arthurian tale, themes from the classics and from folk-lore, oriental tales, sermons with *exempla* and without, and the huge and perennial discussion in *Melibee* on the merits of violence and non-violence, so familiar to us all, make up a wide catch of home and foreign fish in Chaucer's English net. If it is a rough truth that the Middle Ages were interested in narrative, and the renaissance in character, here in *The Canterbury Tales* was the first meeting-place of those two epochs. It was a work that held the past and looked forward into the future.

The poetical qualities of *The Prologue* and the links between tales differ from those of the tales themselves in many ways, though not in all, nor at all times. But in general the latter are dominated by fantasy and speculation and are as much (but no more) removed from *The Prologue* as a man's imagination is removed from his appearance. Together they body forth the civilization of the fourteenth century as seen in sunlight and domesticity. That it could be seen in other ways, as Langland saw it for instance, was no concern of Chaucer's. He chose to measure the world by its smiling self rather than by the Kingdom of Heaven. More than this, his yardstick was in a sense homely and private. Although a courtier at the geographical centre of politics, he found no material for poetry in the major national events of his times. Plague, schism, the Peasants' Revolt, and the clashes between Richard II and his Nobility, that were to end in deposition and regicide, have no place in his poem of England. Jack Straw's massacre of the Flemings in 1381 was poetically no more to Chaucer than the flurry in a farmyard roused by the rape of Chanticleer.

This homeliness is apparent in his imagery. It is the imagery of common sight and sense, achieving the poetry of fact. He has a steady, effortless power of making what seem to be prose statements gleam and glow as they never do in prose. His similes are for the most part the obvious ones of common conversation, though none the less charming for that:

> Whit was his berd as is the dayesye . . .

> His eyen twynkled in his heed aryght,
> As doon the sterres in the frosty nyght . . .

> As hoot he was and lecherous as a sparwe . . .

> As leene was his hors as is a rake . . .

But imagery as we know it in Shakespeare, Donne, Milton, or Keats, the imagery of broken opalescences, half-tones, imprecise suggestion, sudden wonder, extended learning, remote allusion and, above all, the imagery of metaphor that shows one thing instantly in terms of another with a flash of revelation, is nowhere to be found in *The Prologue*, and rarely if ever in the rest of Chaucer's work.

Yet, in a more primitive sense of the word, *The Prologue* is nothing but a series of images, pictures of things directly present to the senses. Shape and colour reach us sharply and immediately, as if from some bright and clearly defined object in life, say a geranium. These bright natural images move to a dance of syllables and to a turn of meaning on the rhyme that give a sudden sharpness of definition, as when the sun comes out on a garden. There is an ever-present liquidness of movement in his language, now unrecapturable in poetry because those gliding terminations that he knew so well how to use have vanished from our language. We can no longer make the music of such a line as

And smalë fowelës maken melodyë

We can make other music, but this kind is lost to us for ever.

A quizzical but affirmative delight in the created world, an eye for the immediate image and an ear for the natural music of speech gathered their forces in Chaucer to express in *The Prologue* his long experience of the daily dealings of men and women. The greatness of his work lies not only in the pleasure of so sharp and happy-hearted a sight of times past, but also in the power it imparts to us to see men and women, our own contemporaries, with a like vision, a like sympathy and amusement, a like intelligence, in their individual actuality. Every reader of *The Prologue* feels he has learnt to open a Chaucerian eye upon the world.

10

TALES AND TELLERS

IN TWENTY-FIVE years of travel, courtiership, civil service, and steady reading, Chaucer had continuously matured his poetical vision and refined upon his dexterity in writing. Every gift of tradition and genius that he had already shown, except two, achieved their perfection of clarity and fullness in the tales and tellers of *The Canterbury Tales*. The two exceptions are his gifts in allegory and tragedy; the dream-vision was at last abandoned, the sustained and intimate pathos of *Troilus and Criseyde* never again reached, save for a moment in *The Knight's Tale* when Arcite goes to his long home.

Every other of his peculiar gifts that we have traced is there, and more came into being, especially the newly sharpened observation of men and women and their behaviour together, new subtleties of story-telling, and new studies in the preposterous. As the *Tales* are a collection, incompletely arranged, of stories written at several periods of his life, and as the basis of their unity is their almost unfailing power to exemplify and expand what we have already been told of the pilgrims that tell them, I have thought it best to single out this aspect of the work, with a little regrouping, so that tales that share certain kinds of vision or quality can be considered together, as well as in relation to those who tell them.

THE KNIGHT

The place of honour fell naturally to the Knight. A long tradition of militant Christianity had gone to form this pattern of authority, humility, candour, and kindness. Medieval Latin for a gentleman was *generosus*, that is, one with a largesse or freedom of nature, believed by some to be hereditary, coming from 'ancient wealth and gracious manners'; an opinion attributed to the Emperor Frederick of Swabia by Dante, in the third chapter of the fourth Book of his *Convivio*. Neither Dante nor Chaucer believed that to be 'gentle', that is, truly *generosus* (free, truth-loving, chivalrous, courteous, magnanimous, considerate for others, *etc.*) was hereditary. In *The Wife of Bath's Tale* Chaucer goes out of his way to deny it. In his opinion the behaviour of a gentleman is achieved by the imitation of Christ:

> Crist wole we clayme of hym oure gentillesse,
> Nat of oure eldres for hire old richesse.

That was the way to keep 'truth', to be 'free', to have *caritas* of heart. Langland would have agreed:

'Whan alle tresores aren tried,' quod she, 'trewthe is the
     best:
I do it on *deus caritas*[1] to deme the sothe . . .
Who-so is trewe of his tonge . . . and telleth none other,
And doth the werkis therwith . and wilneth no man ille,
He is a god bi the gospel . agrounde and aloft,
And ylike owre Lorde . . .

(Piers Plowman, B Text, Passus I)

And indeed there is much that is godlike in the Knight, as there is in Duke Theseus, the dominating character of his tale and of *A Midsummer Night's Dream*. Many an English Manor has bred such men, and they reach in our literature from this one to Sir Roger de Coverley and

---

[1] I prove it by 'God is Love'

beyond. He was a soldier as well as a Christian by profession, having 'foughten for oure feith at Tramyssene', and his tale has all the colours of heroic chivalry, seen through a soldier's eye. His style of narration is one of easy conversational rhetoric, tinged with humour, appropriate to his own nobleness as to that of his story, colloquial without vulgarity and elevated without pomp. There is nothing cold in his courtliness and nothing mean in his homeliness. The style derives, as does the tale, from Boccaccio; we have already seen something of it in *The Parliament of Fowls*

> Besekynge hire of merci and of grace,
> As she that is my lady sovereyne;
> Or let me deye present in this place.

These are the words of the royal tercel, but they would come as naturally from the lips of the woeful Palamon.

Chaucer's handling of the *Teseide*, his source for *The Knight's Tale*, is like his handling of *Il Filostrato*, the source of *Troilus and Criseyde*. He has cut out a great deal, thrust in imaginations of his own, and cast a stronger colour of the rigours of courtly love upon the tale. The deliciously absurd debate (on which Arcite's final defeat and tragedy depend) as to whether Palamon or he has technical priority as the lover of Emilia, is Chaucer's invention, as is the nobly chivalric passage in which the two friends arm each other in silence for the mortal combat that is interrupted by the Duke:

> Ther nas no good day, ne no saluyng,
> But streight, withouten word or rehersyng,
> Everich of hem heelp for to armen oother
> As freendly as he were his owene brother;
> And after that, with sharpe speres stronge
> They foynen ech at oother wonder longe. . . .

One of the marks of Chaucer's narrative power, seen
everywhere from his earliest works, is a genius for wise
digression. He can add a sudden philosophical depth to
any story by an impulse to ponder what it is that makes
things fall out the way they do. He cannot tell so much
as the story of a farmyard fox without invoking Predestination. So, in *The Knight's Tale*, he is moved by the
story to comment on that human blindness that begs its
own destruction unwittingly:

> Infinite harmes been in this mateere.
> We witen nat what thing we preyen heere:
> We faren as he that dronke is as a mous.
> A dronke man woot wel he hath an hous,
> But he noot [1] which the righte wey is thider,
> And to a dronke man the wey is slider. [2]

As a man of tournaments, the Knight was well versed
in the building of the Lists. So was Chaucer from his
experience in the Office of Works, and all that power of
static description that we first saw in his picture of the
Temple of Fame is spent in this story on the splendid
details of the Lists built for the battle of Arcite and
Palamon, with the appropriate temples of Mars, Venus,
and Diana. For his power to describe action, already
seen in his legend of Cleopatra, we have only to turn on
to the battle itself:

> Ther shyveren shaftes upon sheeldes thikke . . .
> Up spryngen speres twenty foot on highte;
> Out goon the swerdes as the silver brighte;
> The helmes they tohewen and toshrede;
> Out brest the blood with stierne [3] stremes rede . . .
> Ther stomblen steedes stronge, and doun goth al. . . .

Lightly accented by alliteration, the passage brings to
eye and ear the heraldic splendour, the tall spears, the

[1] But he does not know.   [2] Slippery.   [3] Stern.

horses in mid-prance, and even the fallen warrior ('he rolleth under foot as dooth a bal') of Uccello's great picture in the National Gallery, *The Battle of San Romano*, dominated by just such another figure as Duke Theseus himself. Poem and painting spring from a like kind of vision, as did *The Book of the Duchess* and *The Hunt at Night*.

In this brief romance-epic, leading from love to battle and back, Chaucer took one touch of humanity from Boccaccio unusual in this type of love-tangle. Emilia, the heroine, has no wish for either lover, having a temperament fully feminine and fully virginal, such as was more often manifest in times when convents were more plentiful than now. Such temperaments still exist, no doubt, but are seldom seen in the heroines of romances. Chaucer, who could understand the Wife of Bath, could also understand one who 'could well endure the livery of a nun'.

The character of Arcite is matched by his doom. Not having been the first to declare his love for Emilia, he had no true claim to be her lover and was a recreant from the Code. For that reason the Gods took his victory from him, and it is only in his death that his real magnanimity is seen to triumph. His last speech is one of a natural nobility, among the finest things in Chaucer, one of the fine things in the whole range of romantic writing; yet, lest it overbalance our feelings, Chaucer tops it with a stroke of wit, if that is not too sparkling a term for an effect of comedy and pathos peculiarly Chaucerian, in the lines describing Arcite's death:

> His spirit chaunged hous and wente ther,
> As I cam nevere, I kan nat tellen wher.
> Therfore I stynte, I nam no divinistre;
> Of soules fynde I nat in this registre.

This imperturbable balance of the High and the Colloquial styles matches the mystery and agnosticism of this moment of poetry.

THE MILLER, THE REVE, AND THE COOK

The High Style, the noble theme and the golden world had found voice in the Knight. Now, in the voices of the Miller, the Reve, and the Cook, we hear the churl-style on the theme of cuckoldry, and enter the world of bum and bumpkin. This was an entirely new vein to tap; nothing he had written up till then gives the least expectation of it. Chaucer the Courtier suddenly reveals the power to create an outrageous and unquenchable cottage laughter.

The spirit of these tales is subtended from his general glee in existence, a joy in the warm energies of nature being itself. The quality of this new poetry can be tasted in a single line, perhaps the funniest line in the funniest story in the world:

'Tehee!' quod she, and clapte the wyndow to.
(The Miller's Tale)

If this is the spirit that propels these stories, it propels them in two contrary directions, harmonized by the miracles of Chaucer's factual style of daily imagery. From one point of view they are totally fantastic, from another rigidly realistic. What is fantastic is the narrative outline; what is realistic, the detail of village life, conversation, and character.

The stories existed for him already in something the same forms and in several languages. There are analogues to *The Miller's Tale* in German, Flemish, and Italian, and to *The Reve's Tale* in Italian and French. These *fabliaux* were for the most part written down in the fifteenth century and for their clumsiness and lack of gaiety seem dull and dirty by comparison with Chaucer, whose style is as clean and as sharp as a whistle. The bare narratives are fantasies of farce, built on a sort of algebra of sex, where x, y, and z of the possible world are made to behave as they could only in theory, and one could write Q.E.D. or 'which is absurd' with equal truth at the end of either tale. This is, indeed, what the Miller and the Reve (parodying his foe) do write. Both tales close with a preposterous summary of their incredible events, though the summary of the Reve piles the whole comic agony on the Miller's head, whereas the Miller had been content to spread the misfortunes of the night impartially among his characters.

But then we had been told in *The Prologue* that no one could get the better of the Reve:

> Ther was noon auditour koude on him wynne.

Injected into and sustaining the narrative fantasy is the acute sense of actual village life. The portrait of Alison, heroine of *The Miller's Tale*, is as sharp and compendious as any in *The Prologue*: hardly less so is that of her priest-lover, Absalom, who combed his hair and played Herod in village theatricals. So, too, in *The Reve's Tale* the two young rascals, Aleyn and John, have a twang of Northern dialect with half a dozen peculiarities of speech confirmed as authentic by the philologists. The Miller shows an equal ease in reproducing village gossip:

> This sely carpenter hath greet merveyle
> Of Nicholas, or what thyng myghte hym eyle,
> And seyde, 'I am adrad, by Seint Thomas,
> It stondeth nat aright with Nicholas.

K

> God shilde that he deyde sodeynly!
> This world is now ful tikel, sikerly.
> I saugh to-day a cors yborn to chirche
> That now, on Monday last, I saugh hym wirche. . . .

The Cook's Tale is unfortunately no more than a brilliant beginning, but it was clearly to have been a piece of town-scurrility as well matched with his character as are the country matters of the Miller and the Reve to theirs. If their tales fill out what we already know of them, their preambles tell us still more, especially the Reve's preamble. Chaucer's sympathy with this creature of his led him to soften and explain the bitterness of the man, so that his nature and point of view grow before our eyes as he meditates aloud on old age and death:

> As many a yeer as it is passed henne
> Syn that my tappe of lif bigan to renne.
> For sikerly, whan I was bore, anon
> Deeth drough the tappe of lyf and leet it gon;
> And ever sithe hath so the tappe yronne
> Til that almoost al empty is the tonne.

The Reve's imagery rises from the things a Reve would naturally have in mind, liquor and forage:

> Gras tyme is doon, my fodder is now forage. . . .

Wordsworth never touched this in his pursuit of the language of dalesmen.

THE MAN OF LAW, THE PRIORESS, AND THE SECOND NUN

The lives of Saints and Martyrs are written for the edification of Christians and to confute, if possible to convert, unbelievers. It is not often that they have any beauty other than the moral beauties of fortitude, chastity, devotion, and the like, for these do not necessarily beget literary beauties. But just as in the hands of a master the crude *fabliaux* of country copulatives can be turned into a subtle uproar of healthy comedy, so the miracles and martyrdoms related by the Man of Law, the Prioress, and the Second Nun are beautified by two rare Chaucerian powers, his sense of pity for the helpless, and his reverence for the Blessed Virgin. Even the least successful of these three tales, that of the Second Nun, has moments of loveliness as in the lines imitated and, as I think, improved from Dante (*Paradiso* XXXIII, 7–9):

> Withinne the cloistre blisful of thy sydis
> Took mannes shap the eterneel love and pees.

And when Tiburce enters the room in which an angel stands with garlands of roses and lilies fetched from Paradise, there is genius in his remark:

> I wondre, this tyme of the yeer,
> Whennes that soote savour cometh so
> Of rose and lilies that I smelle heer.

But the Second Nun, as is perhaps right, cannot compare with her Prioress as a story-teller, nor can she speak so well of visionary things:

> O martir, sowded [1] to virginitee,
> Now maystow syngen, folwynge evere in oon
> The white Lamb celestial . . .

She too has stanzas in veneration of the Virgin, towards which indeed her whole story tends, that recall Chaucer's earliest poetry, the *A.B.C. of the Blessed Virgin*:

O mooder Mayde! or mayde Mooder free!
O bussh unbrent, brennynge in Moyses sighte,
That ravyshedest doun fro the Deitee,
Thurgh thyn humblesse, the Goost that in th'alighte.[2]

(Prologue to The Prioress's Tale)

[1] Confirmed in.
[2] Who, by thy humility didst ravish down from the Deity the Spirit that alighted in Thee.

Chaucer's touch with children (as also in the story of
Ugolino in *The Monk's Tale*) has an unselfconscious
sweetness. Unaware of such a thing as sentimentality,
he cannot be said to avoid the pitfall, but rather that an
instinct of simple and untainted tenderness guides him
through and beyond danger, all the more securely because he seems not to know there is a danger:

> 'And is this song maked in reverence
> Of Cristes mooder?' seyde this innocent.
> 'Now, certes, I wol do my diligence
> To konne it al er Cristemasse be went. . . .'

Her story warms and enlarges the account given of her
in *The Prologue*, and seems to spring from the line

> And al was conscience and tendre herte.

When called upon for a tale, she laid her other femininities
aside, forgetting her little vanities in grave dedication to
her theme.

There seems to be no congruence between the Man
of Law and his tale, though they could not be said to
be absolutely at war with each other. It seems almost
certain that Chaucer at one moment had intended him
to tell some other story, for in his preamble he promises
something 'in prose'. It has often been argued, and I
think reasonably, that when he wrote this preamble,
Chaucer designed to let him tell *The Tale of Melibee*,
replete as it is with learned argument consequent on the
commission of a crime. At some later stage, Chaucer
conceived the joke of getting himself interrupted for
incompetence, and so invented his *Tale of Sir Thopas*,
its collapse, and his modest insistence on the right to be
heard. Then fell *Melibee* upon their ears, his 'litel thing
in prose'. If this is what occurred, the Man of Law

would have been left with a preamble but no story, and
so the tale of Dame Custance, probably written some
time before, was unearthed and attached to him without
care for the discrepancies. Chaucer could no doubt have
smoothed them out if he had lived to complete his whole
design.

The Man of Law's preamble is amusing for its grave
celebration of Chaucer's eminence as an Ovidian story-
teller. No one in the company seems aware that the author
he is praising with such tolerant condescension is present:

> . . . That Chaucer, thogh he kan but lewedly
> On metres and on rymyng craftily,
> Hath seyd hem in swich Englissh as he kan . . .

His tale vies with that of the Prioress, for although the
narrative outline, taken from Nicholas Trivet, is weak
and repetitive compared to that of the tale of the little
chorister, the treatment rises to greater and more varied
poetical heights. There is no stanza in *The Prioress's Tale*
to match in force that in which the Man of Law describes
the situation of his heroine by a sudden comparison with
one of the daily and dreadful sights of fourteenth-century
London:

> Have ye nat seyn somtyme a pale face,
> Among a prees, of hym that hath be lad
> Toward his deeth, wher as hym gat no grace,
> And swich a colour in his face hath had,
> Men myghte knowe his face that was bistad,
> Amonges alle the faces in that route?
> So stant Custance, and looketh hire aboute.

This and other fine things in the poem, such as the
five stanzas beginning:

> Men myghten asken why she was nat slayn?

the verse of rhetorical apostrophe, that seems addressed to the Court assembled round the poet:

> O queenes, lyvynge in prosperitee,
> Duchesses, and ye ladyes everichone . . .

and the tender stanzas leading into the prayer of Custance to the Virgin, her Patroness, beginning:

> Hir litel child lay wepyng in hir arm

are none of them in the sources from which he took the tale.

Chaucer tells us that after *The Prioress's Tale*,

> Whan seyd was al this miracle, every man
> As sobre was that wonder was to se.

These three Tales were told and listened to as triumphs of Christianity, and a willingness to be moved by faith, prayer, and miracle is a condition of their full enjoyment. Simple pathos and the sufferings of the helpless are a great part of their beauty, but there is also the beauty of holiness and of Christian triumph which helped to sober their first hearers, and the astounding strength of the language of prayer:

> Victorious tree, proteccioun of trewe,
> That oonly worthy were for to bere
> The Kyng of Hevene with his woundes newe,
> The white Lamb, that hurt was with a spere. . . .

An imagination able and willing to be kindled by such things is necessary to an understanding of these poems. Those who find difficulty over them may at least approach these miracles like those who in a poem of Hardy's went out on Christmas Eve into the stable to see whether (as legend asserted) they would find the cattle on their knees, and hoping it might be so.

THE CLERK OF OXFORD

This unworldly, unbeneficed scholar, seeming himself
to be a lost cause among the ecclesiastical successes of
his fellow-pilgrims, and yet 'ful of hy sentence', that is,
of elevated thoughts, is the only proper pilgrim to tell
the tale of Patient Griselda, whose patience is so high
that Chaucer felt constrained to take it down a little
at the end of the story, where for the only time in *The
Canterbury Tales* he openly usurps the mouth of a character to confute him:

> Grisilde is deed, and eek hire pacience,
> And bothe atones buryed in Ytaille . . .

The Clerk in proud but quiet reminiscence tells us
he had the story from Francis Petrarch himself at Padua.
Whether or not we are to read Chaucer for the Clerk in
this grand moment of his life, the Tale of Griselda certainly comes through Petrarch, from Boccaccio. It is one
in which every stanza is richly, carefully written, with sober
feelings of conscious compassion and conscious artistry:

> Amonges thise povre folk ther dwelte a man
> Which that was holden povrest of hem alle;
> But hye God somtyme senden kan
> His grace into a litel oxes stalle. . . .

As a story it is perhaps a little long for what it has to tell.
But this is not the secret of the uneasiness that some feel
in reading it. It is too cruel, too incredible a story.
J. Burke Severs in his article on the poem in Bryan and
Dempster's *Sources and Analogues of the Canterbury Tales*
says it is of folk-lore origin, and I am indebted to Dr. R.
M. Dawkins for referring me to Emmanuel Cosquin's
Contes Indiens et L'Occident where that origin is to be found
in the widely diffused oriental folk-tale of *The Ogre*

Schoolmaster. Here are seen the tested heroine and her surrendered children, and at long last their miraculous restoration to recompense her patience. By seeing what has happened to the story in the hands of Boccaccio, Petrarch, and Chaucer, we can to some extent account for the uneasiness that the incredibility and cruelty create. In a word, they have sought to humanize it; they have built it into a circumstantial history of personal relations exemplifying the virtue of absolute wifely patience and submission. And that is what sticks in the gorge. Even Chaucer could not stand it and had to write his marvellously versified ironical disclaimer.

Whatever archetypal notion, if any, underlay the original folk-tale, whether, perhaps, it has something to do with the idea of waiting for luck to turn in a wicked and irrational world, I do not know. But certainly *The Ogre Schoolmaster* is neither so heavily personal nor so heavily moralized. Nor does he live in the detailed, possible world of actuality, as we are asked to believe Griselda did. The humanism of Boccaccio has been applied to material that cannot bear such a load. Italy is not Ogre-land, the old wine of folk-tale has a harsh taste in the modern bottle, and what was meant as magical has become monstrous. Not all Chaucer's delicacy of diction or power of compassion where womanhood and children were concerned could rescue the tale. Renaissance moralizing and sophistication have ruined a simple ogre-story.

It is generally thought to have been written not long after Chaucer's first Italian journey; I would conjecture that when he came back to it for inclusion in *The Canterbury Tales* he felt as we do about it. Even its attribution to the unworldly Clerk, who knew nothing of women

except that obedience was demanded of them in marriage, could not soften it enough. So Chaucer added his
ironical tail-piece some fifteen years after having translated the story itself, in his maturest vein of wit and
rhyming ingenuity.

> Ye archewyves, stondeth at defense,
> Syn ye be strong as in a greet camaille;[1]
> Ne suffreth nat that men yow doon offense.
> And sklendre wyves, fieble as in bataille,[2]
> Beth egre as is a tygre yond in Ynde;
> Ay clappeth as a mille, I yow consaille.

THE WIFE OF BATH

All but one of Chaucer's portraits are clear and bright
like profiles on a sunny day. Their subtlety does not lie
so much in the character as in the way in which character
is described. There are no tormented souls, split personalities, freaks or enigmas. No Hamlets, no Heath-
cliffs, no Judes, not even a Don Juan. But to all this
Alison, the Wife of Bath, is an exception; she is large and
contains contradictions.

Among the great comic figures of our literature, Falstaff is her only match, and it is a great pity that Shakespeare, wishing to show Sir John in love, threw him away
on Mistress Page instead of turning, as he so often did, to
Chaucer, to find in the Wife (Sir John's contemporary,
after all!) a mate of equal wit and will. What dialogues
are lost to us!

She is in every way remarkable. Even in *The Prologue*
she appears as an assembly of details more striking than
any other; yet Chaucer held most of her character in
reserve and it is not until we reach the preamble to her

[1] Camel.
[2] And slender women, feeble in battle, be fierce as a tiger.

tale that the fullness of her personality swells that startling outline and makes more than good the first summary
of her essentials. We then see it was right that she should
have stood out so violently in *The Prologue*; there was no
one with such a force of life in all the cavalcade.

Her preamble is the first autobiography in English
fiction. It discloses a nature violently coarse and derisive,
thoughtfully theological and in a sense religious, very
restless, very overbearing, amazing in her self-knowledge,
yet blind as to whether it is love or power that she is really
seeking. She is very feminine, and very comic, yet there
are touches of tragedy in her defiant comedy. Worldly
as she claims to be, she is still a restless soul. What was
she doing, looking for husband after husband, seeking
shrine after shrine?

She had a considerable scrap-heap of personal learning, sacred and profane, pressed into the service of her
remarkable opinions and way of life. Her candour and
energy make one believe she could have worn five husbands out and battled her way so often across Europe,
to Spain, to Italy, and to the Holy Land, in the intervals
of making cloth and making love.

Vivid as might be her stockings, they were less vivid
than she. She had been the battle-ground of Experience
and Authority, and, like Chaucer her creator, had given
due heed to both. She begins her preamble with the
latter. Christ, she said, reproved the woman of Samaria
for her five husbands, and for the man she had that was
not her husband, but

> What that he mente therby, I kan nat seyn. . . .
> How manye myghte she have in mariage?
> Yet herde I nevere tellen in myn age
> Upon this nombre diffinicioun.

There was the example of Solomon to consider, and Saint Paul had laid it down that it was better to marry than burn. And where in Holy Writ was virginity commanded? It may have been counselled,

> But conseillyng is no comandement . . .
> And certes, if ther were no seed ysowe,
> Virginitee, thanne wherof sholde it growe?

It seemed unanswerable. Later, in *All's Well That Ends Well*, Parolles was to use the same argument.

Moreover every vessel in a great house is not made of gold; she was content to do good service as a wooden platter. Again, for what purpose were the instruments of generation made? For the mere purging of the body?

> The experience woot wel it is noght so.

Yet though she holds it fit that her experience should override some authorities, she admits that of Christ, 'that of perfeccion is welle':

> Crist was a mayde, and shapen as a man,
> And many a seint, sith that the world bigan;
> Yet lyved they evere in parfit chastitee.
> I nyl envye [1] no virginitee.
> Lat hem be breed of pured whete-seed,
> And lat us wyves hoten [2] barly-breed.

And so she passes to the next point in her case, her will and power to subjugate her husbands:

> I have the power durynge al my lyf
> Upon his propre body, and noght he.

---

[1] I think the meaning is 'say nothing against' in this context.   [2] Be called.

Of her five husbands she says that three were good and
two were bad, and she reached her judgement thus:

> The three were goode men, and riche, and olde;
> Unnethe [1] myghte they the statut holde
> In which that they were bounden unto me. . . .
> As help me God, I laughe whan I thynke
> How pitously a-nyght I made hem swynke!

She actually taught them to be grateful to her when
she spoke them fair, having great skill in humiliating
dialogue. All the sarcasms and tricks that smart in
a husband's ear were at her command, from the open
rebuke

> Thou comest hoom as dronken as a mous

to sulking over a forgotten birthday. She had the nerve
to cast their counter-attacks in their teeth, as one who
picks up a live grenade and flings it back before it bursts.
Her subtlest technique went even further; she invented
things for them to say against her, and said them first.
There was nothing left for them to say:

> Whoso that first to mille comth, first grynt; [2]
> I pleyned first, so was oure werre ystynt. [3]

No parry like a thrust:

> I swoor that al my walkynge out by nyghte
> Was for t'espye wenches that he dighte; [4]
> Under that colour hadde I many a myrthe. . . .

So it was with her 'good' husbands. Her fourth and fifth
she handled differently, according to their natures:

> My fourthe housbonde was a revelour;
> This is to seyn, he hadde a paramour.

---

[1] With difficulty.
[3] So our war was stopped.
[2] Grinds first.
[4] Kept.

She was still young (she had married first at twelve years old), and 'ful of ragerye'; so she retorted her jealousy upon him:

> That in his owene grece I made hym frye
> For angre, and for verray jalousye.
> By God! in erthe I was his purgatorie,
> For which I hope his soule be in glorie.

He died on her return from Jerusalem and she buried him simply under the rood-screen.

> It nys but wast to burye hym preciously.

Yet it was at that funeral that she made her great blunder; she allowed herself to fall in love. She had met Jankin, a young Oxford student, boarding with a neighbouring gossip, and all one Lent, while her husband was in London, she had strolled the fields with him. But it was not until the funeral of her fourth that she inwardly capitulated:

> As help me God! whan that I saugh hym go
> After the beere, me thoughte he hadde a paire
> Of legges and of feet so clene and faire
> That al myn herte I yaf unto his hoold.

She was forty, he was twenty, and she loved him. It was fated, for her planets had taken a hand against her. Venus and Mars were in control and she was no longer mistress of the artillery of sex,

> For certes, I am al Venerien
> In feelynge, and myn herte is Marcien . . .
> I folwed ay myn inclinacioun
> By vertu of my constellacioun.

Now, for the first time, a tragic feeling rises to the surface out of the undercurrents of her preamble. Chaucer has the same intuition of her plight as Villon was to have

of the plight of the *Belle Heaulmière*. Her man beat her
and she loved him.

> Now of my fifthe housbonde wol I telle.
> God lete his soule nevere come in helle!
> And yet he was to me the mooste shrewe;
> That feele I on my ribbes al by rewe,[1]
> And evere shal unto myn endyng day.
> But in oure bed he was so fressh and gay. . . .

Only Chaucer and Shakespeare can compound a poetry
in which comedy takes its strength from tragedy. Villon's
Heaulmière utters a lament; The Wife of Bath utters a
manifesto. Her story ends in triumph, but not before she
has come very near to disaster.

Jankin, her young husband with the pretty legs, tired
of her. The truth was that she could not relinquish her
old habits, even under the influence of her new love:

> Stibourn I was as is a leonesse,
> And of my tonge a verray jangleresse. . . .

After many rebukings that had no effect, he retired into
the literature of misogyny, and would read aloud, as he
sat over the fire, all the historic treacheries of women
from Eve onwards, flinging proverbs at her to follow up:

> 'A fair womman, but she be chaast also,
>   Is lyk a gold ryng in a sowes nose.'

Alison at last could stand it no longer. Snatching three
pages out of his cursed book, she smote him on the cheek.

> That in oure fyr he fil bakward adoun.
> And he up stirte as dooth a wood [2] leoun,
> And with his fest [3] he smoot me on the heed
> That in the floor I lay as I were deed.

---

[1] In a row.   [2] Mad.   [3] Fist.

There was a trifle of description, the first thing told of her, far back, in *The Prologue*:

But she was somdel deef, and that was scathe.[1]

That detail, that had seemed no more than a picturesque touch of irrelevance, now is seen as the legacy of her only love, for it was the blow that he struck that had robbed her of her hearing:

> By God! He smoot me ones on the lyst,[2]
> For that I rente out of his book a leef,
> That of the strook myn ere wax al deef.

It was the penalty of Mars and Venus. Perhaps no moment in all Chaucer's poetry shows more subtlety of art and understanding. The story of their reconciliation after this episode is the story of how she got what she says all women want, sovereignty in love. And she got it by a trick.

This woman is driven by two contrary hungers, for love and for power, and that is the secret of her restlessness. When she has power it is no love, and when she achieves love, her power is gone; but there is left her femininity; she has the woman's ace to play even when all the cards are on the table. Her final victory over Jankin has an element of intuitive stratagem, an extraordinary mixture of ruse and passion, impossible in a man.

Yet an analysis of the Wife of Bath on the matrimonial plane alone is not enough, it is too simple. For what drove her so many times overseas on so many dangerous pilgrimages? Why is she now on yet another pilgrimage,

---

[1] That was a pity.　　　　[2] Ear.

and still waiting for another man, in spite of what she calls the 'sorrow and woe' there is in marriage?

> Welcome the sixte, whan that evere he shal!

There was no response to this offer from among the pilgrims. Not one was ready to swim where five had drowned before. Great as was her hunger for power, her hunger for love was still greater, and this is at the root of her restlessness and of that religiousness in her, so startling a bed-fellow to her concupiscences. She has much of the Margery Kempe in her, that strange and maybe mad woman of the next century, also a traveller to distant shrines, also at some time distracted by lust. Margery Kempe had visions of Our Lord; not so Alison of Bath, yet she obscurely felt some pull of Heaven's magnets, as well as the world's. There is a note of defiance in her triumphs, as if those triumphs had not been quite complete:

> It tikleth me aboute myn herte roote.
> Unto this day it dooth myn herte boote [1]
> That I have had my world as in my tyme.

She remains, like Falstaff, the sort of enigma that seems perfectly acceptable and natural. In the Wife of Bath and the Prioress, Chaucer has drawn two characters of perfect and opposed femininities, representative of womankind as the pilgrims are representative of England.

Her tale is built about the mystery of what it is that woman really wants, and it supplies her solution, upon which she had attempted to build her life.

[1] It does my heart good.

> Wommen desiren have sovereynetee
> As wel over hir housbond as hir love.

The tale is an *exemplum* of all she preached and practised.

But apart from its hand-to-glove appropriateness to the Wife of Bath, the story is a notable example of Chaucer's skill in narrative. As she turns from her autobiography to her tale, the style changes from that of racy argument and reminiscence of the most collo-quial kind, to a steady, decorative and highly pointed manner, and every climax is carefully concealed and withheld until the right moment for discovery. There are digressions and delayings, masterly ingredients that set the tone, stay the denouements, heighten expectation, and sharpen the point.

Of many, perhaps the best is the link of decorative irony she makes between the Arthurian world of the tale and the world of Hubert the Friar, her companion in pilgrimage. Hubert had laughed at her preamble; she did not deign a direct reply, but started off her story of Arthurian England that in those times was 'fulfild of fayerye'. But now (she says) no one sees elves any longer, for the Friars with their holy prayers and bless-ings all over the country

> maketh that ther been no fayeryes.
> For ther as wont to walken was an elf,
> Ther walketh now the lymytour hymself . . .
> Wommen may go now saufly up and doun
> In every bussh or under every tree;
> Ther is noon oother incubus but he . . .

and this deft, unforeseeable turn to her tale not only revenges her upon the Friar but also, by another sur-prising twist, leads straight into the main action of her story. While the image of an incubus is still fresh in our

L

minds, the swift narrative tells us of an Arthurian knight,
who, overtaking a girl one morning by a river,

> By verray force, he rafte hire maydenhed.

And thus both ends of her digression are neatly knitted
into her tale.

Chaucer prided himself on the Wife of Bath, as we can
see from his poem to Bukton. He had pondered her
deeply, rejecting one story which I think he had origin-
ally intended for her (but gave to the Shipman), because
the story of the Loathly Lady which she tells was so
much more her own.

CHAUCER HIMSELF AND THE NUN'S PRIEST

The 'murye wordes of the Hoost to Chaucer', and the
consequent tales of *Sir Thopas* and *Melibee*, leave the
modern reader the richer by two jests and an enigma.

The first jest, the jest of Simpleton Chaucer, pops up
in its best and final form, after so many preliminary
sketches from *The Book of the Duchess* to *The Legend of
Good Women*. On each previous occasion it had had a
slightly new twist, echoing the earlier. So now the
plumpness of the poet, adumbrated in *The House of
Fame*,

> Me caryinge in his clawes starke
> As lyghtly as I were a larke,

is matured into the full fun of fatness and combined with
the notion of Scipio Africanus in *The Parliament of Fowls*
that Chaucer would never do as a lover and that he is
dull of wit. The Host addresses him:

> This were a popet in an arm t'enbrace
> For any womman, smal and fair of face.

His dullness of wit is shown by his incompetence as a story-teller; his 'verray lewednesse' in telling *The Tale of Sir Thopas* cannot be endured, even by Harry Bailey:

'This may wel be rym dogerel,' quod he.

The second jest is one of the few in Chaucer that need a learned note for a full taste of their flavour. It is a jest at the expense of the popular romance; *Sir Thopas* is the first as it is one of the most brilliant and subtle parodies in English. To have invented the art of parody in letters is a claim in itself. This kind of parody is criticism in its creative-destructive form. Parody of a kind existed before, in action at least, on occasions such as the Feast of Fools, that New Year buffoonery of Churchmen, when the smoke of sausages and puddings was swung up for incense as the burlesque anthem resounded:

> *Orientis partibus*
> *Adventavit Asinus*
> *Pulcher et fortissimus.*

But the kind of parody brought off by Chaucer in *Sir Thopas* is a piece of cunning literary mockery of current popular taste, even to the variations in the verse-forms sprinkled through the first 'fit', scrupulously copied in derision from current models. As for the matter, the inane tedium of such tales, apart from their doggerel dance of syllables and rhyme, is faithfully mocked, as anyone who can bring himself to read such romances as *Sir Isumbras*, *Sir Eglamour*, or *Sir Percival*, in the collection known as *The Thornton Romances*, can perceive. The pungent silliness of Chaucer's poem is but their dreary silliness in sharper form, as may be seen by comparing two

stanzas from *Sir Thopas* with a snatch from the 1,904 lines
of *Sir Degrevant*:

> He koude hunte at wilde deer,
> And ride an haukyng for river
>   With grey goshauk on honde;
> Therto he was a good archeer
> Of wrastlyng was ther noon his peer,
>   Ther any ram shal stonde.
>
> Ful many a mayde, bright in bour,
> They moorne for hym, paramour,
>   Whan hem were bet to slepe;
> But he was chaast and no lechour,
> And sweete as is the brembul flour
>   That bereth the rede hepe.
>
>   (*Sir Thopas*)
>
> Now to fforest he ffounde [1]
> Both wyt horne and with hound,
> To breying [2] the deere to the ground
>   Was hys most glew; [3]
> Certus wyff wold he none,
> Wench ne lemone, [4]
> Bot as an anker [5] in a stone
>   He lyved evere trew.
>
>   (*Sir Degrevant*)

But I have found no imbecility to equal Chaucer's
inspired

> And I yow telle in good certayn,
>   He hadde a semely nose.

One of the inmost secrets of parody, as can be learnt
from Aytoun's *Firmilian*, is to achieve bathos by the
incorporation of genuine poetry in a context of nonsense,
and this is a trick perceived by Chaucer, as the lines
about the bramble flower suggest.

[1] Rode off.   [2] Bring.   [3] Pleasure.
[4] Mistress.   [5] Anchorite.

The enigma is *Melibee* and its reception by the Host. Are we to think it a contribution seriously offered by Chaucer, as it was accepted by the company? Its immense length, though he describes it as 'a litel thyng in prose', its portentous place in the comedy of his interruption, and what we have seen of Chaucer's love of a private joke at the expense of his audiences as well as of himself, incline me to think that the chuckle it causes was intended by Chaucer. Yet it is possible to argue that moral disquisitions of the kind were common at the time, and would have seemed neither funny nor tedious to anyone, not even to Chaucer. He had, after all, translated this work in all seriousness many years before (so it is believed). It is a question whether we can divine his taste to have changed.

Before we abandon *Melibee* as a bore, it is well to reflect that it is no more than an argument in which we ourselves have so frequently and fulsomely indulged during the last thirty-five years. How many a promising conversation has begun with the gambit 'What would you do if you saw your sister being raped by an enemy soldier?', and how often has this exciting question led to dreary and interminable arguments on the merits of violence and non-violence, often less learned and logical than those of *Melibee*!

Speaking of rape, Chaucer was himself appealed, that is 'accused', of rape by one Cecilia Chaumpaigne; the matter was settled out of court in May 1380. Most Chaucer scholars have hopefully supposed that this 'rape' was no more than an abduction such as that suffered without ill effect by his father in 1326. Medieval law is a matter for legal rather than for literary experts, and the latest opinion, that of Mr. P. R. Watts, published in the *Law Quarterly Review* (October 1947), inclines, for good reasons, to the view that it was indeed rape, *violentus concubitus*, that Cecilia had charged Chaucer with. Later she withdrew the charge, whether true or false. Let us hope Philippa Chaucer bore the scandal with as much philosophy as Dame Prudence in her judgement on the rights of vengeance:

'Lo, lo,' quod dame Prudence, 'how lightly is every man enclined to his owene desir and to his owene plesaunce! . . . For Senec seith, "He overcometh in an yvel manere that repenteth hym of his victorie." Wherfore I pray yow, lat mercy been in youre herte . . . .'

If any one tale could be chosen to show the quintessence of Chaucer's wit, gaiety, and learning, *The Nun's Priest's Tale* would be a fair choice. I incline to think Chaucer at first intended to tell it himself, before he hit on the joke of having himself interrupted as an incompetent, for the story of Chanticleer and Pertelote would have suited no pilgrim so well as himself. He gave it to one of the three priests in attendance on the Prioress whose characters he had avoided describing in *The Prologue*. It may be that he wished to leave himself some blank cheques, in case he should find himself with a story that suited none of the filled-in characters. If so, his foresight was justified; the Nun's Priest comes to life through the story he tells, and he fits well into the entourage of a Prioress so fond of animals.

Dreams, matrimony, and predestination are three of the great Chaucerian themes, and here, in this Aesopian fable, they reappear in a new variation, with learning in their train, both philosophical, medical, and literary. The learned bird of science, seen in *The House of Fame*, no longer an eagle, but now a hen, has an up-to-date knowledge of laxatives. As J. L. Lowes has pointed out, the 'wormes' that she prescribes to the ailing Chanticleer are not simply a remedy to fit a fowl, but the actual medicine recommended by Dioscorides for the human ailment of a tertian ague, from which, she claims, he is suffering. Chaucer's jokes often grow richer as one looks at them. Very few have died.

The hint for a dream comes in what may have been one of Chaucer's sources for this story, the *Roman de Renart*, but in that version, Pinte, the wife of Chanticleer, interprets the dream prophetically, not medically. Chaucer knew more of matrimony than that. It is the husband that would have high pretensions about the significance of his dreams, the wife who would pour the cold water of common sense upon them. And the wife would be wrong:

> Wommennes conseils been ful ofte colde;
> Wommannes conseil broghte us first to wo,
> And made Adam fro Paradys to go. . . .
> But for I noot [1] to whom it myght displese,
> If I conseil of wommen wolde blame,
> Passe over, for I seyde it in my game . . .
> Thise been the cokkes wordes, and nat myne.

This is a part of one of those digressions that are almost the chief beauties in this enchanting tale. Another is when at the breathless moment of the rape of Chanticleer, out comes the organ stop of *exclamatio*,

> O destinee, that mayst nat been eschewed!
> Allas, that Chauntecleer fleigh fro the bemes!
> Allas, his wyf ne roghte nat of dremes!
> And on a Friday fil al this meschaunce . . .

and the digression on Destiny leads to another on the

[1] I do not know.

rules of rhetoric, so exquisitely illustrated in this very
passage, and followed almost instantly by yet a third of
amplificatio :

> Certes, swich cry ne lamentacion,
> Was nevere of ladyes maad, whan Ylion
> Was wonne, *etcetera.*

The comic use of rhetoric and learning are among the
ingredients of this tale at which every reader laughs,
whether he knows of medieval medicine and rhetoric, of
Dioscorides and 'Gaufred, dere maister soverayn' or
not, Gaufred de Vinsauf, author of the *Nova Poetria*,[1] put
here to such loving and preposterous use by Chaucer. I
have counted over four-and-twenty learned allusions to
different authors in this farm-yard story, and one might
almost say that Chaucer's source for it was not the *Roman
de Renart* so much as a life-time of delighted reading and
natural observation. It is as full of reading as an egg is
full of meat, whipped into the lightest of omelettes. And
after all the images that bubble out of books, there comes
the rough and tumble of the immediate vision of a farm-
yard in fugue:

> Ran Colle oure dogge, and Talbot, and Gerland,
> And Malkyn, with a dystaf in hir hand;
> Ran cow and calf, and eek the verray hogges,
> So fered for the berkyng of the dogges . . .
> They yolleden as feendes doon in helle;
> The dokes cryden as men wolde hem quelle;
> The gees for feere flowen over the trees;
> Out of the hyve cam the swarm of bees. . . .

---

[1] This work is a comprehensive treatise on the rules of
rhetoric. There is hardly a paragraph in all Chaucer that
does not exemplify one or more of these rules. See J. M.
Manly's Warton Lecture *Chaucer and the Rhetoricians.*

In Ely Cathedral there is a misericord on the north side of the Choir, carved with a Chanticleer upon a fox's back, with a large woman in pursuit brandishing a distaff. She is Malkin, sure enough. For all his learning, Chaucer could chime in with popular traditions of art, even if *Sir Thopas* is a genial satire on one of them.

THE MONK

Little need be said of the Monk's interrupted series of 'tragedies', except that they seem for the most part early work, in Chaucer's first Boethian and Italian manner, and that they show, on a tiny scale, the germ of a tragic form seen in full perfection in *Troilus and Criseyde*, and, under the hand of Shakespeare, in *Romeo and Juliet*. The Monk is careful to define the form in his preamble and in the first stanza of his Tale. Among the 'tragic' stories that he tells, there is one masterpiece, the tale of Ugolino, taken from the dreadful story in Dante's *Inferno*, cantos xxxii-xxxiii. Chaucer has softened it with all the pity of his nature.

It is sometimes argued that these doleful stories are out of keeping with the Monk's character as we know it from *The Prologue*. But what we know of the Monk in *The Prologue* is gathered by Chaucer in a friendly conversation with him. The Monk, not wishing, perhaps, to be taken by a plump and genial man of the world for a narrow cloister-bounded bigot, boasted a little of his modern opinions, extracting Chaucer's wished-for if ironical approval. But now, when called upon for a tale, the atmosphere is different; he has to defend not his broad-mindedness, but his dignity and that of the

Monastic Orders. Harry Bailey had flung at him publicly the taunt:

> Thou art nat lyk a penant [1] or a goost . . .
> I pray to God, yeve hym confusioun
> That first thee broghte unto religioun!
> Thou woldest han been a tredefowel aright. [2]

Thus it was the changed situation that called forth the changed appearance of character, and we know more of the Monk rather than less, by his response to the demand for a story. While taking that taunt 'al in pacience', he would let the whole company know he was a learned man, with a hundred formal tales of tragedy at his command. And though he may be thought a feeble poet by comparison with some of his fellow-pilgrims, his last phrase about the Goddess Fortune, however much derided by the Host in the discussion that follows, is up to the standard of *Troilus*:

> For whan men trusteth hire, thanne wol she faille,
> And covere hire brighte face with a clowde.

The Boethian notion that the cause of all tragedy is the fickleness of Fortune is not a sufficient motivation even for the 'Tragedies' told by the Monk. The first of them, that of *Lucifer*, is not brought about by Fortune, for, as the Monk tells us, Fortune cannot injure angels, and Lucifer fell from sin. *Sampson* fell telling his secrets to a woman, *Nabugdonosor* and *Balthasar* for being enemies to God, *Antiochus* for pride and so on. But the treatment of these as tragic motives is rudimentary. In so far as Chaucer had tragic vision, it was a vision of pity, and sometimes of irony, but not of terror.

[1] Penitent.   [2] A tread-fowl, i.e. a fornicator.

THE PARDONER, THE FRIAR, AND THE SUMMONER

One of the most striking things about *The Canterbury Tales* is the enormous accession of new interests and energies, producing new styles to contain them, such as we have seen in the tales of the Miller and the Reve and in the autobiography of the Wife of Bath. While these retain or advance the characteristic powers of his earlier work, the sharp intelligence, the conversational dexterity, the learnedness, and so forth, they would have been departures in poetry unpredictable in 1386.

Three other of his new interests are manifested in all that concerns the Pardoner, the Friar, and the Summoner, that religious basilisk and those rival caterpillars. They are his interest in rogues, ecclesiastics, and preachership. His studies in roguery are by no means confined to the Church, but are spread generally among the lower orders, instance the Miller, the Shipman, and the Canon's Yeoman, and the professional classes have a taste of it too. But he has taken special care over these three ecclesiastical rogues and their sermons, which fit them so well that no interchange would be possible. For the Friar and the Summoner he has created a comedy of contempt, bordering in the case of the Summoner on hatred. His full comedy of hatred is reserved for the Pardoner, who is the centre of an ironic rather than a satiric vision. Fielding has some observations in the Preface to *Joseph Andrews* that help to clarify the principles underlying these kinds of comedy :

'The only source of the true Ridiculous (as it appears to me) is affectation. . . . Now, affectation proceeds from one of these two causes, vanity or hypocrisy; for as vanity puts us on affecting false characters, in order to purchase applause; so hypocrisy sets us on an endeavour to avoid censure, by concealing our vices under an appearance of their opposite virtues. . . . From the discovery of this affectation arises the Ridiculous, which always strikes the reader with surprise and pleasure, and that in a higher and stronger degree when the affectation arises from hypocrisy, than from vanity; for to discover anyone to be the exact reverse of what he affects, is more surprising, and consequently more ridiculous, than to find him a little deficient in the quality he desires the reputation of.'

The Friar and the Summoner have their vanities and hypocrisies and are made ridiculous enough, each in an appropriate degree. The Summoner is made to seem hateful even, but not importantly so; satirical exposure of the kind described by Fielding was a sufficient annihilation. But the basilisk Pardoner was more to be feared and therefore more to be hated. A monster of vanity and hypocrisy, he had a wider field of operation within the Church and a still deadlier technique. Pondering him, Chaucer moved beyond simple satire into irony, the most baleful form of militant poetry. In all that he says of the Pardoner he shows himself the first and subtlest ironist in English, for there are ironies within the irony.

The root principle of this figure of rhetoric is that the intended meaning is the opposite to that expressed in the words used, as in Swift's *A Modest Proposal*. Chaucer has used this in *The Prologue*:

> But trewely to tellen atte laste
> He was in chirche a noble ecclesiaste.

In such a mood the Lord commended the Unjust Steward. By an extension this principle can also be applied to situation, and this Chaucer does in the

Pardoner's sermon. The Three Rioters, seeking Death in order to slay him, find him without knowing that it is he, and are themselves slain by their own motive principle, cupidity. The personal situation of the Pardoner himself is equally ironical. It has often been said he is a lost soul, but he is more; he is a lost soul peddling a fake salvation for other souls, as if all salvation were a fake. Like Iago he knows all the right things to say, and says them for his private ends. The irony is that they are true while he supposes them a mockery:

> For myn entente is nat but for to wynne,
> And nothyng for correccioun of synne.
> I rekke nevere, whan that they ben beryed,
> Though that hir soules goon a-blakeberyed!

He has taken the root of all evil to be his good; as the Maiorcan proverb has it, he is seeing black white.

But Chaucerian irony has a quality that I miss in Swift's and beyond the power of this root principle of opposition between what is said and meant or what is done and intended. It is the quality of doom, the sense that there are Higher Powers that see our wishes and doings and know them to be contrary to our own interests but congruent with Their quite other purposes for us. We are blind, but they see. And Chaucer lets us see them seeing. The power to do this arises from his long interest in the notion of Destiny, of 'simple' and 'conditional' necessity,[1] that he had so often argued. What is more ironical than a will supposed free, freely

---

[1] e.g. *Simple Necessity*: all men must die. *Conditional Necessity*: if you *know* a man is walking in your garden, then he must be. Your knowledge does not make him do so, but if you *know* he is there, then he is. So with God's foreknowledge of the Future. (This example is from Boethius, Bk V, Prose vi).

struggling to attain a preordained doom, the opposite of its intention?

> We witen nat what thing we preyen heere.
>
> *(The Knight's Tale)*

As early as in *Troilus and Criseyde* this theme is sounded. In that poem, over which there broods a fatal destiny, the Trojan Parliament clamoured for the return of Antenor, in exchange for Criseyde; Antenor, who was later to betray their city. They freely chose the doom the Gods had preordained for them. So in the ironies of the Pardoner and his tale there is a weaving sense of the supernal powers at work, and his sermon, given in the classic form of Text, Argument, *Exemplum*, and Exordium, is as much a figure of his own doom as of the Three Rioters. God is not mocked.

Nor indeed was Harry Bailey. Though Chaucer does not show us the doom on the Pardoner's hypocrisy, he lets us see a nemesis on his vanity. Confident of his spell-binding as he was (and a little drunk), he had bared the secrets of his profession in his preamble, sure that a sermon that had never failed would work the trick again. He preached it with unction and gusto. It ought to have worked, and with a true strategist's instinct he turned at the end of his peroration upon the most difficult of his hearers. If Harry Bailey collapsed, then all the rest were his. Harry Bailey did not collapse, but voiced the feelings of all England towards Pardoners in his annihilating retort. For once the Pardoner had met defeat.

> This Pardoner answerde nat a word;
> So wrooth he was, no word ne wolde he seye.

The Friar's Tale arises not so much out of what *The Prologue* says of him, though indeed it shows all the suave eloquence there promised, as out of the course of pilgrimage during which he and the Summoner had picked a quarrel. It is a piece in Chaucer's maturest vein of bland anecdote, and shows what a master can do with a chestnut, for the bare bones of *The Friar's Tale* were well known, a commonplace *exemplum* of the importance of Intention when invoking God, in this case specifically with regard to curses. In the mouth of the Friar this theme is artfully blended with his main concern, a sermon on the final destiny of Summoners in general and of his fellow-pilgrim in particular, unless, as we may hope (a Parthian shot), God allows him to repent :

> And with that word this foule feend hym hente ;
> Body and soule he with the devel wente
> Where as that somonous han hir heritage.
> And God, that maked after his ymage
> Mankynde, save and gyde us, alle and some,
> And leve thise somonours goode men bicome !

The tale is full of lively and intelligent conversation, such as only Chaucer can handle in rhymed verse, of which the most remarkable passage, perhaps, is that in which the Fiend tells of the powers allowed by God to him and his associates in Hell. Seldom can the subtleties of theological speculation have sounded so gay and easy.

Although this story is not among the most famous of *The Canterbury Tales*, it has a naturalness, economy, and scorch seldom found outside De Maupassant. And there are individual flashes of wit that make use of the couplet as of a separate hand-grenade casually flung, as Dryden was to fling them, in the course of a general attack :

> He was, if I shal yeven him his laude,[1]
> A theef, and eek a Somnour, and a baude.

---

[1] If I am to give him his due praise.

The Friar had confidently taken the risk of the Summoner's retaliation, and his confidence was justified, for although in his reply he rose splutteringly to such heights as he was capable of, he lacked the trenchant art of the Friar. The bludgeon, not the rapier, was his weapon; or perhaps a blunderbuss, loaded with filth. He was at home in ordure.

Compared with the Friar the Summoner is not only a churl, he is a blunderer. His scattered attack has none of his adversary's educated concentration. He looses off his first barrel well enough, telling of the habitat of the Friars in Hell, and then turns to the second, the story of the strange bequest of poor Thomas to the Friars; this has an analogue in *Li Dis de le vescie à prestre* [1] of the wandering scholar, Jacques de Baisieux, which Chaucer may have known. If so, he redesigned it for the Summoner.

As long as he keeps strictly to his narrative, the Summoner has as great a talent for picturing cottage life as the Miller or the Reve. After driving away the cat the Friar in his story sits down to a lively conversation with the bed-ridden Thomas and his wife in the best vein of village gossip. It is only when he enters upon his long sermon to Thomas that he seems to lose grip. The sermon covers too many subjects; he begins with abstinence, goes on to alms-giving and the duty of patience. This is followed by a disquisition on anger and drunkenness and finally he returns to alms-giving once more with a direct demand for a contribution from Thomas. This leads to the whole point of the story (in so far as it is meant to heap derision on Friars) in the monosyllabic reply that is Thomas's strange bequest.

Considered as a sermon it is lively reading, but con-

[1] *The Story of the Priest's Bladder.*

sidered as a retort to the Friar's sermon it lacks finesse
and bull's-eye aim. Thus the Summoner's lack of art is
a sign of art in Chaucer, for it is fitting that a Summoner
should be less intelligent than such a Friar as Hubert was.
And yet it may be that the Summoner was trying to put
into the mouth of the Friar in his story a parody of what
might normally be expected of a Friar, and that the
sermon is deliberately ill-constructed. It may be a part
of the Summoner's satiric intention to satirize the preach-
ing of Friars as well as the Friars themselves. We are
not told if it was, but there is at least one touch that
recurs in the tale which strongly suggests an intention to
parody the friarly approach to his victims, in the repeti-
tion, maddening to poor Thomas, of his name:

'O Thomas, *Je vous dy*, Thomas! Thomas!...'
'Thomas, Thomas! so moote I ryde or go...'

and so on.

But what the Summoner can do best is neither parody
nor sermoning, but building up a picture of country life;
the excellent scene in the cottage of Thomas is only half
of what he has painted by way of social history. The
other half is to be found at the other end of the story
when the indignant Friar goes to dine with the local
Lord of the Manor. The conversation there between the
Friar, the Lord, his Lady and the ingenious Squire
brings a Great Hall before one with an artistry that
is Chaucer's rather than the Summoner's. We do not
meet with such a scene of life in a great family except in
The Merchant's Tale. These are the moments when the
Chaucerian eye sees farther than we can believe his
creatures capable of, into the comic poetry of contemporary life in being.

M

THE SQUIRE, THE FRANKLIN, AND THE MERCHANT (WITH
    SOMETHING OF THE SHIPMAN)

I have grouped these three together, arbitrarily
perhaps, because they show the imaginations of a young,
a middle-aged, and an old man in the matter of love. It
may be that the Franklin, whose beard we were told in
The Prologue was daisy-white, was no younger in fact
than the Merchant. But the tales they tell do not arise,
as so many do, from their characters as given in *The
Prologue*, but from what Professor Kittredge has discerned as the Marriage Debate, initiated by the Wife of
Bath and concluded by the Franklin as to the seat of
authority in wedlock. It may be that Chaucer had such
a debate in mind as an organizing element in his
enormous poem, but, if so, I think it a part of a still
larger, less precise approach to the whole question of
love-making, in which so many pilgrims have their say,
even to the Miller and the Reve. Chaucer had always
prided himself as the poet of love and love-tidings. The
question of sovereignty in marriage is only one aspect,
however debatable, of so large a human interest. No
English writer, not even Shakespeare, has so varied an
approach to the epiphanies of sex.

The boy's approach made by the Squire is in full
conformity with his character as given in *The Prologue*.
Like Chaucer himself at that age, he was captivated by
the romance delicacies of the courtly code, and the
second part of his tale (the first is introductory) is of a
falcon deserted and betrayed by her tercelet lover, much
as if the formel eagle of *The Parliament of Fowls* had been
deserted by the royal tercel that the Goddess Nature had
advised her to marry, or as if one of the legends in *The
Legend of Good Women* had been the legend of a good bird.

These lines might well be of Jason in the Legend of Hypsipyle and Medea, but they come from the Squire:

> Right as a serpent hit [1] him under floures
> Till he may seen his tyme for to byte,
> Right so this god of love, this ypocrite,
> Dooth so his cerymonyes and obeisaunces,
> And kepeth in semblaunt alle his observaunces
> That sownen into gentillesse of love.

The young Squire is charmingly self-conscious about his style (which is like his father's, unmatured),

> Myn Englissh eek is insufficient,

but his head is full of wonders, horses of brass, magic mirrors, rings, and swords. There is no knowing how long he would have wandered among such age-old, everfresh imaginings, had he not been interrupted by the Franklin. He was still in the tapestry world of Chaucer's own youthful vision. Chaucer had passed beyond it into the common light of day, but it was a world he had never forgotten and could still recapture as if he had never grown old.

The Franklin's Tale is also a romance with magic in it and told in those easy ten-syllabled couplets that mark these later years of Chaucer's writing. These, with *The Wife of Bath's Tale* (not her preamble) and *The Merchant's Tale* are alike in being romances on the edge of fairyland. Rocks are removed by incantations, ancient crones found in the woods turn into lovely girls, and private gardens are visited by Pluto, king of 'fayërye'. Romantic love is their central theme, and 'whylom' their characteristic date. Except for *The Squire's Tale*, which seems to some extent in a deliberately earlier manner, these

[1] Hides.

stories give the norm of Chaucer's maturest style of
courtly narration, the language of gentlefolk. It may be
that *The Shipman's Tale* might be added to the list. It
certainly does not fit the Shipman. All are in a world of
comedy and happy endings, and together they create a
golden world which nevertheless admits of considerable
misbehaviour.

In judging the style of these poems to be more mature
than that of *The Legend of Good Women*, it can be the case
that situation for situation their styles are the same; for
instance

> That he hath reft hire of hire maydenhede
> > (*The Legend of Philomela*)

and

> By verray force, he rafte hire maydenhed
> > (*The Wife of Bath's Tale*)

But because the human situations in the Legends have
less freedom and variety, Chaucer was less often prompted
in them to those turns of wit and sudden moments of
vision, coming to him from his own familiar world that
he seemed better able to identify with 'whylom', than
with the more alien world of a Thisbe or a Cleopatra;
there is something restricting in such a martyrology.
Thus, though every line in the *Legend* is well made, yet
we never come upon such a piece of writing in them as
the opening lines of *The Shipman's Tale*:

> A marchant whilom dwelled at Seint Denys,
> That riche was, for which men helde him wys.
> A wyf he hadde of excellent beautee;
> And compaignable and revelous was she,
> Which is a thyng that causeth more dispence
> Than worth is al the chiere and reverence

> That men hem doon at festes and at daunces.
> Swiche salutaciouns and contenaunces
> Passen as dooth a shadwe upon the wal.

Wit and imagery as in the second and last lines quoted seem to be released by his satirical theme. We have seen him capable of high seriousness, but not of dead seriousness.

The extraordinary tone of sympathy-in-mockery he achieves towards January in *The Merchant's Tale*, by which the old man appears helpless, romantic, generous, tragic and a silly if not nasty old man simultaneously, is an effect of writing that calls forth a double and contrary truth about him throughout the tale, and is especially evoked by the imagery in this passage:

> Heigh fantasye and curious bisynesse [1]
> Fro day to day gan in the soule impresse
> Of Januarie aboute his mariage.
> Many fair shap [2] and many a fair visage
> Ther passeth thurgh his herte nyght by nyght,
> As whose tooke a mirour, polisshed bryght,
> And sette it in a commune market-place,
> Thanne sholde he se ful many a figure pace
> By his mirour . . .

or, later, when poor old January has gone blind and is in process of being cuckolded by a wife he deeply loves,

> O Januarie, what myghte it thee availle,
> Thogh thou myghte se [3] as fer as shippes saille?

The Merchant's Tale is Chaucer's farthest reach into this kind of poetry, and almost every effect his previous works had attempted seems to be present in a final form, touch by touch. It vies with *The Nun's Priest's Tale* as the most 'Chaucerian' story in the work. Although the old man

---

[1] Inquisitive perturbation.   [2] Shape.   [3] See.

who tells it expressly disclaims it as autobiography, no reader can escape the thought that he is speaking of his own experiences a little less directly than the Wife of Bath. The bashful and illicit love of Damian, familiar now in Chaucer's work, expresses itself in a poem that he carries in a silk purse next his heart; for all his quick behaviour in the pear-tree, he is a romantic figure in his own opinion. So is his 'faire fresshe May' in hers; they are as romantic in their thoughts as they are cynical and treacherous in their doings. The garden of their adultery is the most beautiful of all Chaucer's gardens, the mansion of January the most splendid of all his mansions, the wantonness the most elegant and outrageous. Again and again Chaucer (in the Merchant's mouth) breaks in with philosophic comment, proverb, or ironical remark:

> A wyf! a, Seinte Marie, *benedicite*!
> How myghte a man han any adversitee
> That hath a wyf? Certes, I kan nat seye.

And there is a heap of learning, which, if it is not to our taste, was very much to Chaucer's. There is more wit, more feeling, more movement, and more surprise, whether in the conversations or the actions, than in any other of the *Tales*, yet of a kind that we have met before. The story leaves a nasty taste, for one likes old January too much to see him so grossly betrayed. He has no more happiness than what Swift allowed to be happiness, to be well deceived. It is a well-balanced mixture of comedy and tragedy until cynicism turns the scale. It is a perfect story for a rich, lecherous, pathetic, newly married, disillusioned dotard to tell.

If a story is to be judged by the taste it leaves, none is more satisfying than *The Franklin's Tale*. For those

interested in the problems of courtly love, and the
reconciliation of that love in faithful Christian marriage,
it is Chaucer's last word and summary. Dorigen accepts
her lover as a husband on condition that in private he
remains her servant

> And for to lede the moore in blisse hir lyves,
> Of his free wyl he swoor hire as a knyght
> That nevere in al his lyf he, day ne nyght,
> Ne sholde upon hym take no maistrie
> Agayn hir wyl. . . .

She in return offers to be a true and humble wife to him,
and in public to respect his authority.

> Thus been they bothe in quiete and in reste. . . .
> Love wol nat been constreyned by maistrye.
> Whan maistrie comth, the God of Love anon
> Beteth his wynges, and farewel, he is gon!

The conditions agreed between Congreve's Mirabel and
Millamant before marriage are somewhat more sophisti-
cated, but tend to a like result. Both are revolutionary.

But I think the tale has had too much attention from this
point of view. How to be happy though married is not
its true theme. The true theme is noble behaviour, how
to be 'free' in Chaucer's phrase, as 'free' as his Knight,

> That fro the tyme that he first bigan
> To riden out, he loved chivalrie,
> Trouthe and honour, fredom and curteisie.

It is the prime virtue of *generosity*. And it is the point
of *The Franklin's Tale* that this is a virtue that can flower
in any walk of life; it is not a class prerogative. Dorigen
has kept her word to Arveragus, her husband. Yet she
has given her word to yield to her lover Aurelius on what
she supposes an impossible condition. The condition is

fulfilled by magic, and she is faced with breaking her
promise one way or the other. So she consults her husband, and he, the first in generosity, bids her fulfil the
promise to her lover because above all things she must
keep truth. And he bursts into tears. She then, sad at
heart, seeks out Aurelius to perform her rash vow. But
Aurelius, hearing all the circumstances, releases her of it:

> Thus kan a squier doon a gentil dede
> As wel as kan a knyght, withouten drede.

And he in turn goes off disconsolate, unable to pay the
magician that had performed the impossible for him by
magic. Who, informed of all that had passed, forgives
him the debt, saying:

> Thou art a squier, and he is a knyght;
> But God forbede, for his blisful myght,
> But if a clerk koude doon a gentil dede
> As well as any of yow, it is no drede!

and the story ends with the question

> Lordynges, this question, thanne, wolde I aske now,
> Which was the mooste fre,[1] as thynketh yow?

THE PHYSICIAN AND THE MANCIPLE

The tales of the Physician and the Manciple seem to
open unexpected eyelets on Chaucer's personal life at
court, particularly that of the Physician. He has just got
into his stride in a description of his heroine Virginia:
she is a girl of unparalleled beauty and moral delicacy:

> And if that excellent was hire beautee,
> A thousand foold moore vertuous was she. . . .

a girl who avoided all occasions of temptation to folly

---

[1] Free, i.e. free-hearted, generous.

As is at feestes, revels and at daunces,
That been occasiouns of daliaunces.

And suddenly the voice of Chaucer seems to break in,
through the voice of the Physician, to address not the
imaginary audience of Canterbury pilgrims, but the
actual audience of the court circle, to whom, as we know,
Chaucer used to read his poems:

And ye maistresses, in youre olde lyf,
That lordes doghtres han in governaunce,
Ne taketh of my wordes no displesaunce.
Thenketh that ye been set in governynges
Of lordes doghtres, oonly for two thynges:
Outher for ye han kept youre honestee,
Or elles ye han falle in freletee,
And knowen wel ynough the olde daunce,
And han forsaken fully swich meschaunce
For everemo: therfore, for Cristes sake,
To teche hem vertu looke that ye ne slake . . .
Looke wel that ye unto no vice assente,
Lest ye be dampned for youre wikke entente.

This outburst can only have been occasioned (it is
thought) by the scandal of a love-affair that flared up in
1386 between the fiery John Holland, half-brother to
Richard II, and Elizabeth, daughter of John of Gaunt by
his first wife, Blanche—the lady of *The Book of the Duchess*.
This girl had had a governess, Catherine Swynford, *née*
Catherine de Roet. She was the sister of Philippa,
Chaucer's wife. Not long after her appointment as governess to the children of John of Gaunt, she and her
employer fell in love, and she became his mistress;
ultimately (in 1396) he married her. But for many years,
Chaucer must have had to live down the reputation of
his sister-in-law as the Duke's mistress. And now, in
1386, her charge, the young Elizabeth, 'came out' at

court and also 'fell in frailty' to the sudden John. Like
governess, like girl. What made things worse was that
she was married already, by a child-marriage contracted
with the Earl of Pembroke. The Earl however obtained
a divorce, and Holland married Elizabeth and took her
abroad to Spain, to let the talk cool off a bit. Her father,
John of Gaunt, was also in Spain at the time, otherwise it
seems scarcely credible that Chaucer would have dared
to administer this public rebuke to his peccant sister-in-
law. He himself was under the Duke's patronage and
may have had to endure the imputation that he owed this
patronage to the frailty of his wife's sister. Anyhow, he
spoke out.

The Maniple's Tale is a sermon against speaking out.
Its moral is *Keep your mouth shut*! It begins what seems to
be another tale of a tricky wife, who yields herself to a
lout of a lover during the absence of her husband, who
was none other than Phoebus. Phoebus kept a pet, a
white crow, that he had taught to speak. When Phoebus
returned, the bird burst out at him with 'Cokkow!
Cokkow!' and reported his wife's behaviour, which it had
witnessed. So far the story seems conventional enough;
but now comes the twist. It is not a story about adultery,
but about tact :

> Ne telleth nevere no man in youre lyf
> How that another man hath dight his wyf;
> *He wol you haten mortally, certayn.*

Phoebus tore off the crow's white feathers, turned it
black and took away its sweet voice; and then he slung
it to the devil; and Chaucer thinks that the best place for
it. The last sixty lines of the poem are a wonderful
reiteration of the same moral, phrased in the elaborate

and forceful figure of rhetoric, known as *conduplicatio*, which repeats and repeats the apostrophizing word, for the sake of an intenser gravity: *Hold your tongue!* is the burden of this song: more than likely Chaucer learnt the wisdom of doing so at Windsor:

> But nathelees, thus taughte me my dame,
> '*My sone*, thenk on the crowe, a Goddes name!
> *My sone*, keep wel thy tonge, and keep thy freend.
> A wikked tonge is worse than a feend . . .
> *My sone*, be war, and be noon auctor newe
> Of tidynges, wheither they been false or trewe.
> Whereso thou come, amonges hye or lowe,
> Kepe wel thy tonge, and thenk upon the crowe.'

THE CANON'S YEOMAN

The episode of the Canon and his Yeoman is the most striking *tour de force* in *The Canterbury Tales*. Beside this achievement the brilliant Envoy to *The Clerk's Tale* with its line upon line and rhyme upon rhyme of irony is a minor miracle. In contrast with the smooth, educated style of the tales just considered, the Yeoman's verses are rough and breathless, the utterance of a sharp but 'lewed' wit. It is a rush of language pouring from a half-instructed mind possessed by his special subject, the impostures of alchemists, in which he has taken his humble part and by which he is driven to a torrent of narrative exposition as if suffering from a variant form of Ancient Mariner's disease.

Alchemy is a subject on which few are qualified in these days to speak, least of all myself. It is certain from the spate of accurate technical terms that tumble helter-skelter from the Yeoman's lips that their jumble is an important part of the comedy; it might be funnier still if we fully understood all their applications and concatenations. The generalized joke is laughable enough, but, trust Chaucer, the detail, did one but understand it, would be better: however,

> To lerne a lewed man this subtiltee—
> Fy! spek nat therof, for it wol nat bee.

The confusion in the mind of this sorcerer's apprentice is comically blent with rage and disappointment, that echoes in the roughness of the versification:

> Oure fourneys eek of calcinacioun,
> And of watres albificacioun; [1]
> Unslekked lym, chalk, and gleyre [2] of an ey,
> Poudres diverse, asshes, donge, pisse, and cley,
> Cered pokkets, [3] sal peter, vitriole. . . .
> This cursed craft whoso wole excercise,
> He shal no god han that hym may suffise.

The sudden and panting introduction of this character and his master (who gallops off again at the threat of exposure) is a piece of actuality devised by Chaucer to break the alternation of tale and link that threatened for all their variety to make a convention of the pilgrimage. The sense of actuality is greatly increased by the fact that this is the only story in the whole collection that has the quality of a contemporary anecdote. There is no 'whylom' about it. It has the eye-witness quality that we have so often seen in Chaucer. Even *The Reve's Tale*, though in a sense contemporary perhaps, is a story he retails from memory for a particular occasion. But *The Yeoman's Tale* bursts immediately out of his personal prepossessions and experiences. No source has been found for this story. It springs from a wedding of

---

[1] 'Of turning water white', as opposed to 'rubifying' or turning it red, another dodge of alchemy.

[2] White of an egg.   [3] Waxed bags.

Chaucer's interests in science and roguery. One of the cheating Canon's conjuring tricks, that of the hollow tube, had made its way into literature before in the twenty-first of the *Novelle* of Giovanni Sercambi, a work that in its construction faintly foreshadows *The Canterbury Tales*, but Chaucer would have had no need of such a source to teach him trickeries that were going on in London at the time, and of which some have thought he may himself have been a victim.

This tale may be called a *tour de force* because of its Kipling-like concentration on an unexpected, technical and specialist's theme that makes a new kind of poetry out of comic jargon conveyed by a sustained character-monologue. It may also be called so for its daring; he took the risk of breaking his framework of pilgrimage to make it more like one than ever. The other pilgrims were fabling to while away their journey. The Canon's Yeoman was bursting with immediate rascalities he could no longer keep to himself. He had to sweat them out of him.

. . . . .

This study has been an attempt to show through twenty-five years of writing Chaucer's gradual mastering of a poetry of comic vision, which although peculiarly Chaucer's is also European, and English especially. As in the work of our other greatest poets, his originality was fed by tradition. What he has left us is the offspring of Authority and Experience, the eldest-born taking more after their mother, the youngest after their father. The fundamental things taught him by the civilization of Christendom, he never lost touch with; they were especially the idea of Gentle behaviour, the quality of Pity, and the delicacy of a romance feeling for natural beauty and the Springtime of the world. These he always

retained while extending his vision beyond an aristocratic setting to include the richer riots of less exalted
people. If these were the factors that guided his intuition,
his intelligence and craft as a poet drew from earlier
models an exact and various sense of the values of syllabic
verse, and a feeling for the forms of narration. All these
things he gathered into the service of his unique personal
powers of wit and observation and applied them to
express and sustain his delight in what is individual in
men and women and the actual world.

The total was a new and perennial comic vision, loved
and shared by Shakespeare. These two poets see and
show a whole society in being, united by common purposes and moving towards a happy end in a dominant
mood of easy goodwill (roguery notwithstanding) where
the whole is made up of diversities, and the individual a
part of it in virtue of being so fully himself. Common
sense and fantasy, wit and pathos, ride side by side and
make the ordinary and the normal unique, touching,
funny, and memorable. And in both poets romantic
love is the core of the comedy.

Both writers seem to lack the 'moral purpose' so palpable in Ben Jonson and other corrective writers of
comedy, in whom satire and self-assurance predominate
over good nature and modesty. Chaucer and Shakespeare seem more concerned with a 'happy' than a
'moral' ending for comedy. Happy endings they certainly do create, and the happiness is transferred from
the characters in their stories to the reader and spectator.
It may well be that the creation of their kind of happiness
is, in the long run, more moral than all that the moralists
can do. *Beatitudo non est praemium virtutis, sed ipsa virtus.*

At the end of *Troilus and Criseyde* Chaucer had prayed

for the might to make something in comic form. His
prayer was answered more fully than he had asked. He
had made comic form itself. He was born lucky. Laughter is difficult to explain philosophically and Comedy is
difficult to define critically. The unhappy dilemma of
the critic is that the harder he tries the more serious he
becomes, and the more serious he becomes the farther he
seems from his subject.

For it turns out that Comedy that seems (in a nutshell)
to be a glimpse of a tufted wart on a miller's nose is,
like Tragedy, a glimpse of a Universe. Tragedy cannot
be discussed without reference to forces held to be
supernal; as Destiny, or Fortune, the Gods, the struggle
of Good and Evil. And it asserts the virtue and dignity
of man. It is a religious form of writing. *And so is
Comedy*, though it asserts man's affectations and frivol-
ities. It is a proverb that the sublime and the ridiculous
are but a step apart, and this was a step constantly and
I suppose deliberately taken by medieval artists: instance
the grotesques and gargoyles in their holy places;
instance Mak being tossed in the blanket for lamb-
stealing by those shepherds to whom in a moment arch-
angels are to announce the birth of the Lamb of God.[1]
The form of Comedy, as of Tragedy, depends on the
slant or direction of a writer's beliefs or disbeliefs, and
that can be subtended to Infinity.

I have refrained from prying into Chaucer's relations
with Philippa, his wife, not wishing to ravel out a secret
he preferred to keep. He also kept the secret of his
religious views, and it may be that I have no business
to intrude on them either. Yet without some conjecture I cannot account either for his Tragedy or for his

[1] The *Secunda Pastorum* in the Wakefield Mystery Cycle.

Comedy, and to do that is a part of my purpose, for they are a part of his poetry.

In Tragedy he accepted the fiction of the Goddess Fortune as presented to him by Boethius. To us it may seem a slender and childlike concept to bear a great weight of thought and feeling, and Chaucer, an instructed Christian, knew just as well as we do that no such Goddess existed. But his experience as well as this revered authority (Boethius) told him that certain things fell out *as if* she existed; and '*as if*' is a firm basis for an imagination. She was something more than a fiction to him in that she personified his recurring moments of predestinarian belief, and he surrounded her with a tenuous theology, at least in his poetry, where she appears or is implied as the Executrix of One higher than herself, of 'Joves', of 'Wierdes', or of 'the Firste Moevere'. So many and so subtle are the passages referring to divine foreknowledge and pre-ordination that, as a poet, his faith may be seen to have a 'kyndely enclynyng'[1] to determinism. And this sense of the inevitable that produced the tragedy of Troilus could lean on the fiction of the Goddess Fortune and give colour to the ironies encompassing the Pardoner.

But although pathos and doom qualify much of his finest writing, his dominant poetical mood is one of delight, no less related to supernal powers. This delight shows itself most frequently on the plane of normal human pleasure, and has kinship with the views he attributed to Epicurus:

> That heeld opinioun that pleyn delit
> Was verraily felicitee parfit.[2]

---

[1] A natural attraction to.
[2] From the account of the Franklin in *The Prologue*.

Yet in this very couplet he implies that of course we all know better than Epicurus, and there is something more than pleasure in a true felicity.

Dante looked at the Universe, saw all his horrors, human and hellish, and waded through them as the necessary road to the Beatific Vision. His poem ends in that final felicity, not in pleasure but in bliss, and at the farthest reach of human utterance such as only Bach has touched in the Sanctus of the B Minor Mass. Dante called his poem a Comedy. It ended happily, better than well.

This is the thing that Chaucer meant us to take for granted in his gentle gibe at the philosophy of the pagan Epicurus. Christianity has extended the realm of human ecstasy to include the supernatural. At the same time it was seldom Chaucer's way to speak directly of such things.

A Swiss cathedral organist once described himself to me thus: *'Oui, je suis catholique, mais pas très aigu'* and I thought at the time how well the phrase would have pleased Chaucer, a catholic but no zealot. He was undoubtedly nourished as a catholic and there is nothing in his work to suggest apostasy, though there are moments of a mild agnostic reserve. On one point, however, he had no doubts, namely the glory of God's creation that included so many wonderful and preposterous things. A phrase I have heard from an Irish pulpit would also, I think, have delighted him: 'And God saw that the world was good. *And God was partly right.*'

I do not quote these anecdotes to raise a laugh, so much as to indicate a way of laughing. Chaucer took joy in the universe, a joy that was craftily qualified by

N

footnotes, certainly, but joy nevertheless. Joy is not an experience often expressed in modern art; Egdon Heath, rather than the garden of the rose, is our idea of a landscape. Without wishing to over-simplify history, I would attribute this not to our wars and political nightmares—Chaucer endured such things too—but to the dimming of the concept of Christendom and of that which ordained it. Anxiety is our characteristic mood. The 'far-off divine event to which the whole creation moves' seems farther off than ever.

Chaucer's joy, whether we can recapture it or not, is the fountain of his comedy. Like Shakespeare's, it expresses itself in harmonies, forgivenesses, bounties, and tolerances. And thus it makes a happiness, which is an image of that final joy, an affirmation and a laughter, because all shall be well. There need be no real anxiety. This comedy of gladness is the most English kind of Comedy, as Chaucer and Shakespeare are the most English of writers. But we have another stream of comic writing that flows less from a doxology than from a commination, a puritan rather than a catholic laughter, corrective rather than affirmative. Ben Jonson and Fielding can use it. Its essence is ridicule, punishment, and ostracism, a desire to change the world and the reader, and it offers an ethic rather than a thanksgiving. These two streams of Comedy can at times mingle; Fielding has his moments of joy, Chaucer his moments of rebuke, but the main currents are distinct in their effort to 'make us alle goode men'.[1]

A story that ends happily is a figure of an ultimate good. The central theme of Comedy for a zealot like Dante is the divine love; for Chaucer, aware of that

[1] *Nun's Priest's Tale.*

bounty but preferring somewhat to limit his gaze, it is the human affections of individual men and women. He shows their lives as a pilgrimage from a public-house to a cathedral, with many tales and adventures by the way, a sermon to cap them, and the promise of a dinner at the end.

SELECTED READING LIST

TEXTS

The Complete Works of Geoffrey Chaucer ed. W. W. SKEAT in 7 Volumes. Oxford 1897.

The Complete Works of Geoffrey Chaucer ed. F. N. ROBINSON. 1 Volume. Cambridge, U.S.A., and Oxford, England, 1933.

Troilus & Criseyde ed. R. K. ROOT. Princeton 1926.

SOURCES

Sources and Analogues of the Canterbury Tales. W. F. BRYAN and G. DEMPSTER. Chicago 1941.

The Story of Troilus. R. K. GORDON. London 1934.

The Book of the Duchess. G. L. KITTREDGE. Publications of the Modern Language Association of America, Vol. XXX No. 1.

TECHNICAL

The Language and Metre of Chaucer. B. TEN BRINK, translated by M. BENTINCK SMITH. London 1901.

Chaucer and the Mediaeval Sciences. W. C. CURRY. London and New York 1926.

Chaucer and the Rhetoricians. J. M. MANLY. Warton Lecture on English Poetry: Proceedings of the British Academy 1926.

Bibliography of Chaucer 1908–1953. DUDLEY DAVID GRIFFITH. University of Washington, Seattle, 1955.

CRITICAL

Five Hundred Years of Chaucer Criticism and Allusion. C. F. E. SPURGEON. Cambridge 1925.

Geoffrey Chaucer. E. LEGOUIS, translated by L. LAILAVOIX. London 1913.

Geoffrey Chaucer. J. L. LOWES. Oxford 1934.

Chaucer. G. K. CHESTERTON. London 1932.

The Chaucer Tradition. A. BRUSENDORFF. London, undated.

Studies in Chaucer. T. R. LOUNSBURY. New York 1892.

A Commentary on the General Prologue to the Canterbury Tales. MURIEL BOWDEN. London 1949.

Chapters on Chaucer. KEMP MALONE. Baltimore, Maryland, 1951.

Geoffrey Chaucer. NEVILL COGHILL. British Council, 1956.

The Parlement of Foules, an Interpretation. J. A. W. BENNETT. Oxford 1957.

Chaucer and the French Tradition. CHARLES MUSCATINE. California 1957.

REFERENCE WORKS

A Chaucer Handbook. R. D. FRENCH. New York and London 1947.

A Chaucer Concordance. J. S. P. TATLOCK and A. G. KENNEDY. Carnegie Institute, Washington, 1927.

Chaucer, A Bibliographical Manual. E. P. HAMMOND. New York 1908.

A Manual of Writings in Middle English. J. E. WELLS. New Haven 1916; subsequent Supplements 1919, etc.

BACKGROUND

The Allegory of Love. C. S. LEWIS. Oxford 1936.

Chaucer and his England. G. C. COULTON. 1930.

The Mediaeval Village. G. C. COULTON. 1925.

English Wayfaring Life in the Middle Ages. J. J. JUSSERAND, translated by LUCY TOULMIN SMITH. 1925.

England in the Age of Wycliffe. G. M. TREVELYAN. 1929.

Chaucer's World. Compiled by EDITH RICKERT. Edited by CLAIR C. OLSON and MARTIN M. CROW. New York and London 1948.

INDEX

(References and allusions to individual Canterbury Tales are given under the names of their tellers, except in the case of Sir Thopas and Melibee, which appear under their own names. For abstract ideas under frequent discussion, see Chaucer, Geoffrey: Some leading Chaucerian subjects.)

187